The Greatest

Command

Complete list of Christian books by Gary Schulz

The Greatest Command
Hope for the Depressed
Become a Biblical Marriage Counselor
May They Be One
Relationships —Why Jesus Came
From God's Perspective
From Victim to Victory
The Discipling Father
Setting the Captives Free
New Wine New Wineskins
God's Creation of the Sexual Union
If You Love Me...
Partners
Saved from our Enemies
Good News of Jesus Christ
Eternal Life What Is It?
God's Creation of Work
The Power Of God's Grace
God's Creation, The Family
Marriage Enrichment
Passing Your Faith
Freedom From Anger
Clearly Seen
Creation to Rebellion to Restoration
Oil In Your Lamp
Wimps!
Controlling Parent Controlling Child
Restoring Broken Walls

The Greatest

Command

Gary Schulz

Kingdom Come Publications
81 Oaklawn Dr.
Midland, MI 48640

Printed in the United State of America

Contents

Chapter 1

Heart, Soul, Mind and Strength

Most people, Christian or not, can recite the Golden Rule: "Do unto others as you would have them do unto you." Although, I suspect that not everyone knows these are Jesus' words as found in Matthew 7:12.

This isn't the only time that Jesus told us how to love others. One time he was challenged to choose the most important commandment, and the Golden Rule was not number one; it ranked number two.

One of the teachers of the law came and heard them debating. Noticing that Jesus had given them a good answer, he asked him, "Of all the commandments, which is the most important?"

"**The most important one**," answered Jesus, "is this: 'Hear, O Israel, the Lord our God, the Lord is one. Love the Lord your God with all your **heart** and with all your **soul** and with all your **mind** and with all your **strength**.' The second is this: 'Love your neighbor as yourself.' There is no commandment greater than these."

"Well said, teacher," the man replied. "You are right in saying that God is one and there is no other but him. To love him with all your **heart**, with all your **understanding** and with all your **strength**, and to love your neighbor as yourself is more important than all burnt offerings and sacrifices."

When Jesus saw that he had answered wisely, he said to him, "You are not far from the kingdom of God." And from then on no one dared ask him any more questions. Mark 12:28-34 (NIV) [In Matthew 22:34-

1

38 Jesus refers to this "most important command" as the "first and greatest command".]

How are we to love our neighbor? We love them as ourselves. That may seem simple, but entire books have been written about what this means. Even Jesus was challenged about this command. One time an expert in the law, who wanted to justify himself, asked Jesus who to regard as his neighbor. So Jesus gave the story of the Good Samaritan, and asked the man to identify the neighbor in the story. (Luke 10:25-37)

So even such a simple command as "Love your neighbor as yourself." is not straight forward. Should we love our enemies? Are they our neighbors? Jesus had to address this one too. (Matthew 5:43-48) So what is my point? Who to love and how to love someone is not so obvious.

What Is Loving God?

So if loving our neighbor as ourselves is not clear in our hearts and minds, what about loving God? What does it mean to love him with all our heart? How is that different from loving him with all our soul? And how does one go about loving him with their mind? And the command is to love with **all** my heart, **all** my soul, **all** my mind and **all** my strength. What constitutes **all**? What does this really look like? If I were to start today, what exactly would I begin to do in these areas?

Loving God is as critical to our faith as any one of our beliefs. It is just as important as believing that Jesus is the Messiah, the Son of God and Son of Man. In fact, Jesus came to restore our relationship with God so that we could love him. (2 Corinthians 5:18-21) Loving God is just as important as believing that Jesus died for our sins. In fact, if we do not love God, the blood of Jesus did not restore our relationship with God; for Jesus came to reconcile our relationship with God. *Our relationship is two-sided. It is a relationship of love. God loves me and I love God. It is a marriage of love flowing both ways—from God to us and from us to God.*

2

Jesus made a very strong statement regarding God's love for us. And I am *not* convinced that most believers in Jesus actually believe what he said about the necessity of our love for him.

> **The person who has my commandments and obeys them is the one who loves me. The one who loves me will be loved by my Father, and I will love him and will reveal myself to him."**
>
> "Lord," Judas (not Judas Iscariot) said, "what has happened that you are going to reveal yourself to us and not to the world?"
>
> Jesus replied, **"If anyone loves me, he will obey my word, and my Father will love him, and we will come to him and take up residence with him. The person who does not love me does not obey my words.** And the word you hear is not mine, but the Father's who sent me. John 14:21-24 (NET)

Think about what Jesus is saying to us. First, if we love Jesus, we will obey his commands for us. We must all ask ourselves, do we love Jesus, which is revealed by our pursuit of living out our lives according to his ways and joyfully obeying his commands. This is not an obedience to gain his love; this is an obedience that reflects our love for him. It is the evidence that we love Jesus. If we do not love him and his ways, we will not pursue his ways. Remember, Jesus did not say that he had the way, or that he had the truth or that he had life. No, he proclaimed that he was the truth, the way and life itself.

> Jesus answered, "I am the way and the truth and the life. No one comes to the Father except through me." John 14:6 (NIV)

To love Jesus is to love each of these aspects of who Jesus is. Jesus continues by proclaiming that the Father loves those who love his Son Jesus. And to those he loves, he will reveal himself to them so that they will know God. He also promises to "take up residence" in those who love him. He will make his home in those who love him.

These statements by Jesus are very serious. Loving God and God loving me is the essence of having a relationship with God. It is not so much about whether I go to heaven or hell when I die as much as it is whether I have a relationship with God before I die so that I will have one with him for eternity. This relationship is based on his love for me and my love for him.

Other Lovers

Loving God means that we love him, and love him without competition for our love. Becoming a Christian requires of us to make a decision: Who do we love? Certainly, we must believe in Jesus for who he is, but that is not enough. James wrote that the demons believe and shudder. (James 2:19) Believing is not the same as loving. We must first believe, but if we do not also love God above all else in life, our beliefs have no relational basis.

Jesus was clear that we cannot love God if we love something or someone more than God. Think about what he said about money.

> No one can serve two masters. Either he **will hate the one and love the other**, or he will be devoted to the one and despise the other. You cannot serve both God and Money. Matthew 6:24 (NIV)

America is one of the wealthiest nations on earth. Money is the major decision maker for most businesses and corporations. When the president of the United States gives his state of the nation address, he usually equates our health as a nation with the health of our economy. Money is a major factor in personal or family decisions. Personal debt is rampant. Money can be our master.

We have to make a very serious choice: Do we love money more than God? Jesus made a very strong statement about the difficulty for the rich to enter the kingdom of God.

How difficult it is for those who have wealth to enter the kingdom of God! For it is easier for a camel to go through the eye of a needle than for a rich person to enter the kingdom of God. Luke 18:24-25 (ESV)

Having money isn't the problem; loving money is. And Jesus is saying that those who have it will have a great struggle against loving it more than God. Money can define who we are in the eyes of man. Money can be our source of security and provision. We can be a slave to money such that we dedicate our lives to striving for it. Remember, keeping the Sabbath Day was simply a matter of not going to work one day out of seven. There was a time in America when stores were closed on Sundays. Now all stores are open. There was a time when we could support a family of four children on one wage earner. Now, with all of our technology, we have declined to a family of two children needing two wage earners to pay for all of our accumulated material wealth. Who is our god—really? Paul warned us about this conflict between loving God and loving money.

But godliness with contentment is great gain. For we brought nothing into the world, and we can take nothing out of it. But if we have food and clothing, we will be content with that. **People who want to get rich fall into temptation and a trap and into many foolish and harmful desires that plunge men into ruin and destruction. For the love of money is a root of all kinds of evil. Some people, eager for money, have wandered from the faith and pierced themselves with many griefs**. 1 Timothy 6:6-10 (NIV)

Money is not the only thing that we can love in this world. It is not the only thing that we can idolize. It is not the only thing that can consume our love and rob God of what belongs to him. We can make an idol out of food. (Philippians 3:19) All addictions are idols: gambling, pornography, sex, drugs, alcohol—they are all worshipped by the flesh of man in replacement of God who is there for all of our needs. Hobbies and sports can become an idol if they distract us from a first priority with God. The Bible speaks of us as God's spouse, and he will not compete with anything in this life that we have raised up as more important than God himself.

Loving God is not something we just say; it is something we do. It is easy to say, "I love you." It is much more difficult to live it. True love is lived. True love is a choice. There is always competition for our love.

Dear children, let's not merely say that we love each other; let us show the truth by our actions. Our actions will show that we belong to the truth, so we will be confident when we stand before God. 1 John 3:18-19 (NLT)

To love God we need to recognize whatever else in our lives is competing for our love for God. What else comes first? What other gods do we have before God himself? God is a jealous god, and he does not tolerate our love for other gods, for people or things above our love for him. He must be first in our love priorities. And these priorities must be revealed in how we actually live. He is a jealous God.

You must not make for yourself an idol of any kind or an image of anything in the heavens or on the earth or in the sea. You must not bow down to them or worship them, **for I, the LORD your God, am a jealous God who will not tolerate your affection for any other gods**. I lay the sins of the parents upon their children; the entire family is affected—even children in the third and fourth generations of those who reject me. But I lavish unfailing love for a thousand generations on **those who love me and obey my commands**. Exodus 20:4-6 (NLT)

As we read through the Old Testament, we see a very clear and repetitive problem: idol worship. There are many attitudes, thoughts and behaviors that grieve our Creator, but idol worship stands out as the one that hurts and angers God most. We may not make statues out of gold or silver and put them up to worship, but we can have many idols just the same. The statue is just an obvious object of worship, but the silver and gold can be worshipped just the same, especially if in the form of money. An idol is anything we worship that we believe gives us security, status, provision, power or anything that replaces who God should be to us in our lives. There are many idols; money is just a major one.

> The idols of the nations are silver and gold, the work of human hands. They have mouths, but do not speak; they have eyes, but do not see; they have ears, but do not hear, nor is there any breath in their mouths. Those who make them become like them, so do all who trust in them! Psalm 135:15-18 (ESV)

Money in itself is not the problem. Trusting in money rather than in God is the problem. We cannot love God and also love money. We cannot have other lovers and then proclaim that we love God. This is absurd as an adulterous wife saying that she loves her husband.

Many idols are deceptive. It would be obvious if we had carved out a statue and bowed down to worship it. But most idols are not so obvious. God created us, and we are totally dependent upon him. He is our provider, our protector, our guide, our strength, our life—he is everything. He loves us, and he desires to have a bond with us as we look up to him as our loving Father who provides all things for us. Idolatry is when—like a runaway child—we seek out to live life in our own strength. Our own abilities can become our god.

> They are guilty; **their strength is their god**. Habakkuk 1:11 (HCSB)

Loving God is not a legalistic requirement. Jesus did not come, die on the cross, rise from the grave and send his Spirit just so we would not go to hell, but go to heaven. He came so that our relationship with God would be restored. *Salvation is all about restoring a love relationship with God; that is why Jesus came. Without a love relationship with God there is no salvation.* He came to save our relationship by saving us from our enemies that are consuming our love for anything other than the one true God.

Think of a marriage. A husband does not want to share his wife with anyone else. An adulterous affair would arouse any husband's jealousy and anger. Even flirting with another man would be playing with his fury. Certainly, his wife could love other people and of course her (his) children. But even with these expected loving relationships, a husband would expect to be her first love. He is to be loved above all else. That is what God expects of our love for him. Jesus could not have been clearer in this regard.

> If you want to be my disciple, you must hate everyone else by comparison—your father and mother, wife and children, brothers and sisters—yes, even your own life. Otherwise, you cannot be my disciple. And if you do not carry your own cross and follow me, you cannot be my disciple. Luke 14:26-27 (NLT)

As stated in these verses, we can put other people ahead of God, but we can also put things ahead of God. It may be possessions, but it could also be our time, our money, our careers, our recreational activities, our status in life, our addictions—anything that we put first over our relationship with God. If God has to compete for anything, it is too high on our priority list. Furthermore, being a disciple of Christ requires of us to give up everything in life in order to follow Jesus.

> So you cannot become my disciple without giving up everything you own. Luke 14:33 (NLT)

Jesus never made it easy to follow him. He never compromised by lessening the requirements. Jesus called a man to follow him, but the man said that he first had to bury his father, but Jesus told him to let the dead bury the dead, but first go and tell others about the kingdom of God. (Luke 9:57-62) Do we love his kingdom more than the world we live in?

Another man wanted eternal life, and he had done many good things in his life. But Jesus told him to go sell all that he had, give it to the poor and then to come follow him. But the man couldn't do it because he was more in love with his wealth than becoming a follower of Christ. And Jesus did not run after him and lessen the requirement. He let him go. (Matthew 16:19-21)

God has a great deal of competition for our love. This world is filled with tempting passions that lure us away from God, who is to be our first love.

> **Do not love the world or the things in the world. If anyone loves the world, the love of the Father is not in him,** because all that is in the world (the desire of the flesh and the desire of the eyes and the arrogance produced by material possessions) is not from the Father, but is from the world. And the world is passing away with all its desires, but the person who does the will of God remains forever. 1 John 2:15-17 (NET)

Jesus gave a parable of those invited by the king to his son's wedding banquet, but many of the invited guests did not come because they had many personal things to attend to instead. One had to plow his field; another had to tend to his business. So the king sent his servants out to invite anyone who was not too distracted by the love of their own things. The originally invited guests were locked out and never enjoyed the wedding. (Matthew 22:1-14) God is looking for a bride for his Son. He is not going to allow anyone to be part of this glorious wedding if they are not fully committed to the marriage.

God's Conditional Promises

We commonly like to quote God's promises for us from the Bible. This is a very good practice. It shows our faith and dependence upon God. But far too often we quote these promises without considering that many are conditional on fulfilling our part of the promise. Read through the beatitudes. (Matthew 5:1-12) These are nine blessings from God, but each one has criteria for us. For example, "Blessed are the merciful, for they will be shown mercy". Or "Blessed are the pure in heart, for they will see God." The Psalms are filled with conditional promises. God makes many promises that are contingent upon us doing our part.

Here is a promise that I have heard others quote more times than I can remember. Maybe you have too. Maybe you have been the one to quote it.

And we know that all things work together for good for those **who love God**, who **are called according to his purpose**, Romans 8:28 (NET)

As many times as I have heard this quoted, it was mainly to proclaim God's part of the promise—that all things would work together for good. The assumption is that this promise is for all who consider themselves to be Christians. It is quoted as though we did not have any conditions to fulfill in order to make the promise come true other than to be a Christian. But take note that this promise is only for those who love God. I suppose that those who quote this promise assume that they love God. But does God think that he is being loved? That is why this book is so important for all of us. We need to know what love for God looks like. We can't just say we love God. We can't just make it some emotional statement. And realize that our love for God is not appreciation or high regard; it's the giving up of our lives for him because he is our highest regard. And notice from this passage that our love for him is connected to being called to live a life according to his purpose. Living for God's purposes is love for God. If we are going to claim God's part of this promise, we need to claim our part in the promise and live it out as well.

Let's consider another conditional promise of God's, another promise that is contingent upon our love for him. Psalm 91 is a powerful psalm for God's protective covering over those who abide in him. This is a covering for enduring in the midst of hardships and attacks due to the presence of the devil's evil upon the earth. It is also filled with promises of God to protect his loved ones in the midst of his wrath upon all his enemies. At the end of the psalm God makes promises to those who love him.

Because he loves me," says the LORD, "I will rescue him; I will protect him, for he acknowledges my name. He will call upon me, and I will answer him; I will be with him in trouble, I will deliver him and honor him. With long life will I satisfy him and show him my salvation. Psalm 91:14-16 (NIV)

To those who love God, he promises to rescue, protect, answer, deliver, honor, give a long life, satisfy and show him his salvation. That's a long list. All we have to do is love God and acknowledge his name. But we need to know what it means to love him if we are to fulfill our part of the promise. How do we love God with all of our heart, mind, soul and strength? We can't claim the promises if we do not qualify. So let's explore the scriptures to find out what it means to love God from his written word to us.

Reflection Questions

List and describe your most important relationships with people (spouse, parents, children, etc.). Describe your love, trust and heartfelt intimacy in each relationship.

Now describe your personal relationship with God in like manner.

What things in your life (outside of people or God) are most important to you? Think of possessions, time, career, money, status, food, addictions, entertainment, sexual pleasure, recreation, hobbies, talents, skills, the way you look or appear, physical security, where you live, travel or anything that is part of this physical world.

Keeping in mind the importance of your priorities in life, where is God in your list of priorities, and what is the evidence?

Chapter 2

A New Soul, Spirit and Heart

Jesus said that the greatest command in the law is to love God with all of our heart, soul, mind and strength. (Mark 12:28-34) But what is our spiritual heart, and how does that differ from our soul? And how does our mind connect with the heart and soul? Furthermore, we are to love with all of our strength. Is that referring to the strength of our bodies, such as our muscles? Or is it referring to our spiritual strength, the ability to persevere—the discipline of making ourselves do something that is difficult? Or is it the giving up of our personal lives for the sake of living for God's will and purposes?

And it gets more complicated. We are living beings with several adjoining parts. We all have a mind, heart, soul and body. And even though they are separate parts, they join together and function as one being. It would not be so mysterious if we could just look into our being and see the different parts working together. It is like a car engine. For the most part, we just get into our cars, turn the key to start the engine, put the car in gear and drive. Many do not know what goes on under the hood. There is a fuel system, cooling system, electronic system, exhaust system, a transmission and other supporting components. We don't need to know the technicalities of each system or how they connect together in order to drive the car. The same can be said for our complex spiritual beings. We can live out each day without understanding how we were made and what goes on inside.

Now suppose—using the car analogy again—suppose that something goes wrong under the hood. Maybe the car won't start. Maybe there is a strange sound or the car lacks power. Maybe the gauges are telling you that the engine is overheating or a "Check Engine" light comes on. Now understanding what goes on under the hood becomes critically important. What do you do? If you know a lot about cars, you may begin to diagnose and fix the problem. But cars have become very complex, and we usually need to take them to a certified repair garage to have a professional with his sophisticated diagnostic equipment, special tools and training.

Similarly, we can live out our lives without understanding the intricacies of how we work inside of our complex spiritual makeup. And if life goes on smoothly without struggles, we may feel that we do not need to know. However, all of us struggle with our lives in one aspect or another. It may be an addiction, and we do not understand what is driving our unwanted behavior. It may be that a relationship has been damaged. Maybe there is stress in our marriage. It is taking its toll, but we do not know how to fix it. Offenses have occurred, and now we must deal with the relationship and the pain and frustrations that exist. We may be struggling with depression, discouragement and lack of hope for the future. We may struggle with worry and fear. All of these, and many more, are spiritual concerns that reside within our spiritual being. Now what do we do? If it was a car, we would go to a mechanic. But what do we do when we are struggling with our life? Do we go to a psychiatrist, a counselor or a pastor for professional help? We might, and that may be what is needed. But our spiritual needs are continuous and lifelong. We can't be forever dependent upon human professional help! And human help is not infallible; it may only put a band-aid on the problem.

We all struggle with something. We can't all go off to a professional with every spiritual need. And keep in mind that the professional has a life of his own that he struggles with. So what do we do on a daily or weekly basis? Fortunately, God has provided a service for us that we can seek in any circumstance, any place and at any time, and his services are free. Let's begin to look at how to avail to his services. First, let's look at the word of

God. It serves as both a diagnostic tool as well as a source for resolving what is wrong. It also serves as a tool for regular life maintenance and better life performance. This understanding of ourselves is critically important for understanding our love for God and how to love him with our whole spiritual being.

God's Word Exposes Our Soul, Spirit, Heart and Motives

When we are in a struggle, we are aware of our thoughts, our emotions and our behaviors, but we are not fully aware of the root cause—what is driving us. The word of God opens us up inside to reveal what is going on— what is truly prompting our thoughts, emotions and behaviors. We are captive to hidden damage and corruption deep inside of our inner spiritual being. Like the car, unless we open the hood and start to expose what is hidden, the problems cannot be diagnosed and the solution will never come. The living word of God opens the hood and shines light on the living parts of our inner being.

> For the word of God is living and active, sharper than any two-edged sword, piercing to the **division of soul and of spirit**, of joints and of marrow, and **discerning the thoughts and intentions of the heart**. Hebrews 4:12 (ESV)

If our intent is to love God with all of our heart, mind, soul and strength, we need to begin to know ourselves and to become spiritually healthy and strong.

> The purposes of a man's heart are deep waters, but a man of understanding draws them out. Proverbs 20:5 (NIV)

The spiritually sick and weak are severely handicapped when it comes to loving God. Jesus came for the sick in heart, mind and soul. The heart is the driving force for good and evil. We were born with sinful hearts that drive us to all sorts of filthy behaviors. Jesus attests to our hearts as the driving force for our behaviors.

> But the things that come out of the mouth come from the heart, and these make a man 'unclean.' For out of the heart come evil thoughts, murder, adultery, sexual immorality, theft, false testimony, slander. Matthew 15:18-19 (NIV)

Jesus came to give us a new heart, to cleanse us from the nature inside of us that is contrary to what it means to love God. Jesus was accused by the Pharisees and teachers of the law that he was hanging out with all of the spiritually dirty people. But Jesus came to heal us and lead us to life.

> Jesus answered them, "It is not the healthy who need a doctor, but the sick. I have not come to call the righteous, but sinners to repentance." Luke 5:31-32 (NIV)

Jesus came to heal us—to change us—from the inside out. Most of the problems and struggles that we experience in our outward lives begin in our inner being. Even how we handle lives struggles begins in our hearts. Even outward struggles such as sickness or poverty are affected by how we act inwardly. And our inward response can be much more serious than our outward condition.

Look at Paul for example. He went through many great hardships. He was falsely accused and sent to prison. He was rejected by many whom he came to help. He was beaten, experienced shipwrecks in the open sea. He was frequently on the run. He did not live in a home, but was dependent upon what God would provide for him on a daily basis. But in all of his outward struggles, he was inwardly content and at peace.

> I am not saying this because I am in need, for I have learned to be content in any circumstance. I have experienced times of need and times of abundance. In any and every circumstance I have learned the

secret of contentment, whether I go satisfied or hungry, have plenty or nothing. I am able to do all things through the one who strengthens me. Philippians 4:11-13 (NET)

Paul found in Christ the ability to be inwardly strong and healthy. Our character comes from our hearts. The heart of our souls drive what we think about, our attitudes, our motives and our behaviors. Our life is in the soul, but the soul derives its life from the heart. The heart drives the actions, but the actions are of the soul.

We have been given the word of God to reveal what goes on in our hearts, our minds and our soul. So much of what drives us inwardly is hidden from our understanding. The word of God opens us up and acts like a window to our soul so we can look in and see what is truly going on. Most of the time we are deceived as to our true motives. For example, we may be struggling with someone else's behavior toward us, and completely miss our own faulty attitudes and thinking inside. In most struggling marriages, the husband blames his wife and the wife blames her husband. And both miss their own major contribution to the struggles in their relationship.

The word of God is powerful. Much of our crippled behavior is due to our perverted and deceptive thinking. Again, it is like the car; it is not operating the way it should, but we do not know the cause, so we just keep driving it, possibly causing more damage. Living with something wrong inside is not life. It is hardly survival. And it is not loving God. The word of God has been given to us so that we would know the truth. The truth reveals. The truth can heal. The truth sets us free—free to love God. Actually, *seeking his truth so that we can become healed and whole inside is loving God.* He loves us and his heart desire is for us to become whole inside. That is why he sent his only Son to die for us—so that we could have his life.

Jesus is the word of God (John 1:1, 1:14). And as the word of God, he transforms us into his righteousness and holiness by his wisdom with a new attitude of our minds.

It is because of him that you are in Christ Jesus, who has become for us wisdom from God—that is, our righteousness, holiness and redemption. 1 Corinthians 1:30 (NIV)

You were taught, with regard to your former way of life, to put off your old self, which is being corrupted by its deceitful desires; to be **made new in the attitude of your minds**; and to put on the new self, **created to be like God in true righteousness and holiness**. Ephesians 4:22-24 (NIV)

Not only can our inner man be sick, wounded and damaged, we live in a sick, damaged and wounded world that is led by our enemy, the devil. We live in a world that lies to us and leads us astray in our thinking. Jesus came to rescue us from the deceptions of the world. Jesus transforms us with his living word so that we see ourselves and all of life differently. We see things as God sees them.

Don't copy the behavior and customs of this world, but **let God transform you into a new person by changing the way you think**. Then you will **learn to know God's will for you, which is good and pleasing and perfect**. Romans 12:2 (NLT)

The Bible is like no other book; it is alive. It is the living word of God that has the power to teach, rebuke, correct, train and transform us into the likeness of God. That is what we all need, and that is love for God.

All Scripture is God-breathed and is useful for teaching, rebuking, correcting and training in righteousness, so that the man of God may be thoroughly equipped for every good work. 2 Timothy 3:16-17 (NIV)

I grew up going to church and Sunday school with my family. But we never read the Bible individually at home. I really had not read the Bible as a whole; I just heard disconnected bits and pieces on Sundays. I was living a very wayward life, and did not know it. Then, at about twenty-nine, I began reading the Bible for myself, on my own. I started with Genesis and over a year read through Revelation. Prior, I had all sorts of beliefs that were not scriptural, but I was unaware of my own deception. Reading the Bible changed my thinking and perspectives, which, in turn, changed the direction of my whole life. I have not stopped reading the Bible on a daily basis since. That discipline began about forty years ago, and the word of God still molds and shapes my thinking, attitudes and behaviors. I love God. And I would not be walking in love for him if not for the work of his word in my life. Jesus is the manna from heaven, the true spiritual bread of life. I eat of him daily. (John 6:32-58, John 1:1, 14)

The Spirit of Truth, Our Teacher and Counselor

We have one more agent from God to reveal what is hidden inside of our complex spiritual being—his Holy Spirit. The Spirit of God is the revealer of truth. He is our Counselor. A counselor is someone who listens to you and attempts to discover what is truly going on inside of you and then he gives you advice as to how to resolve your struggles. All human counselors are fallible. They cannot actually see into you; they predict what is going on by your outward evidence. But the Spirit of truth sees right into our soul. In fact, the Spirit has been given to us to live within us on the inside where all of these struggles truly take place. The Spirit is the true Counselor. And not only does he see everything that goes on inside, he gives perfect counsel. All we need to do is listen to him and follow his directives.

> If you love Me, you will keep My commands. And I will ask the Father, and He will give you another **Counselor to be with you forever. He is the Spirit of truth.** The world is unable to receive Him because it doesn't see Him or know Him. But you do know Him, because **He remains with you and will be in you**. I will not leave you as orphans; I am coming to you. John 14:15-18 (HCSB)

This was God's plan for our salvation from the beginning, to give us his Spirit and his word. God knew that we needed a spiritual heart transplant, and he accomplished it through Jesus Christ. Hundreds of years before Jesus' birth, God told us of the new heart he would give us.

> And I will give you a new heart, and I will put a new spirit in you. I will take out your stony, stubborn heart and give you a tender, responsive heart. And I will put my Spirit in you so that you will follow my decrees and be careful to obey my regulations. Ezekiel 36:26-27 (NLT)

The true circumcision is not of the body, but of the heart. God is not looking for those who obey laws and rules; he is looking for those who have a new heart that desires to live as God would have us to live out of our love for God and all of his ways.

> No, a true Jew is one whose heart is right with God. And true circumcision is not merely obeying the letter of the law; rather, it is a change of heart produced by God's Spirit. And a person with a changed heart seeks praise from God, not from people. Romans 2:29 (NLT)

So there we have it. God has given us his written living word to reveal what is hidden and to transform our thinking and attitudes, and he has sent his own Spirit to live within us as our internal Counselor. We no longer need to be in the dark about what is going on inside us. We now have access to the brilliant light of God who can light up every dark place within us.

> Your eye is the lamp of the body. When your eye is good, your whole body is also full of light. But when it is bad, your body is also full of darkness. Take care then, that the light in you is not darkness. If, therefore, your whole body is full of light, with no part of it in darkness, it will be entirely illuminated, as when a lamp shines its light on you." Luke 11:34-36 (HCSB)

If we are going to love God with all of our soul, with all of our heart, with all of our mind—with our whole life—then we need to know ourselves. We need to understand the individual parts of our created being. We need to make sure that we are not trying to drive our lives with the brakes on or with a powerless engine. Seeking to be like God in how we think, in our attitudes and how we act out our lives is love for God. It begins here. We are fallen beings in a dark world, and much darkness resides within us. *Coming out of darkness where God can work in us is love for God.* He is the only one who can really do it. He is the only one who understands and can divide our soul, heart and mind. He is the only one who understands and can reveal the source of all of our attitudes and motivations. *Hiding from God in darkness is the opposite; it is hatred for God; it is evil.* Here is how Jesus described it.

> This is the verdict: Light has come into the world, but men loved darkness instead of light because their deeds were evil. Everyone who does evil hates the light, and will not come into the light for fear that his deeds will be exposed. But **whoever lives by the truth comes into the light, so that it may be seen plainly that what he has done has been done through God**." John 3:19-21 (NIV)

God will do it, but we need to come out into his light and invite him in. He wants to do heart surgery, but we must be willing to enter the operating room and subject our lives to the master surgeon. Do we trust him with our lives? Are we willing to undergo the changes he will make in us? Do we love the surgeon for who he is and what he will do in and through us? He loves us and he wants us to be whole inside. If we love God, we will invite him to enter into the deepest parts of our lives. We will submit our lives to him out of our faith in him as a loving, all-wise and all-powerful God. What does this mean for us? It means that we will seek out his word with the intent of applying what is revealed to us to our lives in the way we think and live. It means that we will listen to the promptings of his Spirit that lives within us and follow his leading. This assumes that we are born again of his Spirit. And if we are not, and if we want to be equipped to love God, we will ask God for his Spirit.

> If you then, who are evil, know how to give good gifts to your children, how much more will the heavenly Father give the Holy Spirit to those who ask him!" Luke 11:13 (ESV)

Reflection Questions

Have you ever struggled with your life? Was the greatest struggle what went on inside your own heart and soul? What was that struggle like? How well do you know yourself—your true motives?

Even if you do not seem to struggle, what drives you and why? Who are you? Do you know yourself?

How has the study and application of the word of God revealed things about yourself? Do you study the Bible? Do you apply what you learn? What have you learned and applied recently?

Are you born again of the Spirit? What has the Spirit revealed to you about yourself? How has he led you, and how have you obeyed?

Describe how you have entrusted your life to God.

Chapter 3

With All Your Soul

Jesus told us that the most important law was to love God with all of our heart, soul, mind and strength. Before we can delve into what it means to love God with our soul, we must determine the essence of our soul. We all witness our minds, in that we think. We witness our emotions. But how do we love God with our heart? And what constitutes our soul? Jesus said that we are to love God with all of our heart, mind and soul. What is the difference? There must be a difference between these three; otherwise, why would Jesus make this distinction? So let's take a scriptural look at the soul and what loving God with our soul may look like.

What Is the Soul?

If you search out what other Bible commentators say, you may find diverse and confusing opinions. These commentators my sound confident and convincing, but is their understanding biblical? The mind, the heart and the soul are all spiritual parts of our living being. We all have each of these living parts that make up our spiritual being. They function together, making it difficult to separate and discern the differences. The Bible does not give us clear definitions describing the differences, but it does refer to each of these members as different. There are numerous verses that refer to the heart and the soul in the same sentence, so we know they are not the same. So let's look at a few references to get some insight into what constitutes the soul. Let's start with the creation of man.

The LORD God formed the man from the soil of the ground and breathed into his nostrils the breath of life, and the man became a **living being**. Genesis 2:7 (NET)

There are two aspects of the creation of man in this verse. Man is both a physical and a spiritual being. The physical part is derived from the elements of the earth. Every part of our physical being is derived from the fundamental chemical elements of the earth. Almost 99% of the mass of the human body is made up of six elements: oxygen, carbon, hydrogen, nitrogen, calcium, and phosphorus. Only about 0.85% is composed of another five elements: potassium, sulfur, sodium, chlorine, and magnesium. Over 60% of our bodies are water.

That is the makeup of our physical being that God created out of these elements. But God did not stop there. He also breathed into man his breath of life, and only then did man become a "living being". This phrase, "living being", is also translated as "living soul" (KJV, ASV) The Hebrew word, "nepesh" is used here for "living being" or "soul".[1] When Jesus said that the greatest commandment was to love God with all of our heart, soul, mind and strength, he was quoting Deuteronomy 6:5. And in this verse, the same Hebrew word for soul (nepesh) is used. So even though Jesus may have been speaking in Greek, he was referencing the Hebrew word for soul, which has been translated into English in several translations as "living being".

So we can conclude that man is made up of both a physical and spiritual being, the body and the soul. They are distinctly different beings that are united together to function as one, but they are still two: body and soul. The soul, then, is the spiritual part of our united spiritual and physical being.

---

[1] Strong's Concordance Hebrew word [5315], nepesh

Plants, Animals and Man

This Hebrew word, "nepesh", is not limited to the creation of man. It is also used in reference to God's creation of "living creatures" or "moving creatures" such as birds, animals and creatures that move along the ground. (Genesis 1:20, 24, 30, 2:19) I think we can all identify that, unlike plant life, an animal has a conscious life. For example, if an animal is hurt, we don't like to see it suffer. But we do not have the same concern for vegetation. We cut the grass, pull weeds, pick fruits and vegetables to eat, and we never think that these plants suffer with conscious pain or concern for what is happening to them. In comparison, we also know that animals are in a constant conscious state of survival. They feel pain. They respond to the fear of man and predators. They consciously compete for survival. Try taking a bone from a hungry dog. Many animals make good companions because they long for our relationship with them. We can identify with their spiritual nature.

In contrast, plants do not have fear nor make conscious choices. They do not form conscious relationships with each other or with man. But in spite of their lack of consciousness, they are still very much alive. Life is a mysterious miracle that we mostly take for granted. A tiny seed can grow into a massive tree. That alone is a mysterious miracle of life. But even though they are alive, they do not have a soul.

Animals are just as much a miracle of life, but with an added dimension; according to the Bible, animals have a soul (nepesh). Man is also an animal with a soul, but he is much more complex than all other animals. Man is distinctly different from all plant life and other animal life. People have emotions, which are the feelings of the soul. Many animals likely have emotions too, but not as complex; and that is about where the soul similarities between man and other animals stop. We have thoughts and the ability to comprehend and make choices and decisions based on logic. Unlike plants, we experience worry and fear, joy and laughter. We can experience disappointment and encouragement, loss and hope, love and hate, success and failure, boredom and enjoyment, fear and safety, contentment and dissatisfaction. The dimensions of the soul are vast—too many to list.

We cannot experience the soul life of animals. They clearly have a life distinct from plant life, but just as obvious, their life is not like man's soul. Man was created in the image of God. This distinction is unique to man alone. Man has the ability and desire to create, unlike animals. Animals, for the most part, are driven by instincts. Some have the ability to learn from their experiences, but most of what they know was programmed into them from the start. For example, the robin knows from instinct how to build a nest, search for worms, feed her young, fly and migrate. Robins did not go to school to learn these things, and all robins live like all other robins. There is no choice in how they live—it's just programmed into their being by their Creator.

Man was not programmed like other animals. We have the ability to plan and make decisions. We can read and write. We have an unlimited ability to create something new. We have a vast ability to communicate. We live in community with others with governmental rule and an economy as we work to serve our various needs with our many individual skills and talents. Most animals grow to maturity and live out an adult life within a few weeks to a year. This is because they have been preprogrammed by God to do so. Unlike animals, humans are not all alike. Our various skills and personalities are endless. Our differences fit together to form an interdependent community. We have families, and, unlike animals, we raise our young to maturity over fifteen to twenty years because we were not preprogrammed like other animals. We mature through a complex learning process over fifteen to twenty years. And even after we leave home, we continue to learn and mature. Our soul life is uniquely and much different from all other animals that also have a soul life.

Eternal Choice for Our Soul

So what can we conclude from these observations? God created us as living beings. We have two parts to our being, our physical bodies and our soul. They both have life and unite together into one living being. The physical body and the soul (spiritual body) do not live separate lives. On the contrary, they live cooperatively together as one living being—even though they are two distinct beings: one being physical and the other spiritual. Even though they work together as one living being, they are still two different beings. There is physical life and there is spiritual life. There is physical death and there is spiritual death. Jesus talked about killing the body as separate from killing the soul.

> Do not be afraid of those who kill the body but cannot kill the **soul**. Instead, fear the one who is able to destroy both **soul and body** in hell. Matthew 10:28 (NET)

Our physical bodies live in a physical world. Our physical bodies as we know them will not inherit the kingdom of God, for the kingdom of God is made up of spiritual beings. This is a mystery to all of us. We live in a physical world with physical bodies. Our bodies are engrossed in the feelings and pleasures of this physical world. But this world is passing away. It is temporary. Our pursuit and our longing should be for the world to come, not the world as we know it.

> Those who use the things of the world should not become attached to them. For this world as we know it will soon pass away. 1 Corinthians 7:31 (NLT)

Jesus talked about saving or destroying or losing our soul. Even though our bodily life and our soul life are united as one today, we live in an existence where the soul is being tugged at from two directions. The physical life tugs one way and the spiritual life tugs another. Eternal life is in the spiritual life. If we allow our soul to live solely for the physical, we will lose our soul. As Jesus said (above), God is "able to destroy both soul and body in hell". *To love God, we must **not** love the things of this physical existence more than the things of our eternal existence with God in his kingdom.*

> For whoever would save his life will lose it, but whoever loses his life for my sake will find it. For what will it profit a man if he gains the whole world and forfeits his **soul**? Or what shall a man give in return for his **soul**? For the Son of Man is going to come with his angels in the glory of his Father, and then he will repay each person according to what he has done. Matthew 16:25-27 (ESV)

We are at a crossroad in this life: Do we live for this world (physical kingdom) or do we live for the kingdom of God (spiritual kingdom). Jesus himself had to choose when tempted by the devil. (Matthew 4:1-11) The devil took him to a high place where he could see the vastness and splendor of the kingdoms of this world. Then the devil told him that he would give him all of these kingdoms if he would just bow down and worship the devil. Obviously, Jesus made the right choice. He quoted from Deuteronomy regarding how we are to worship God and serve him only. This is really the issue for all of us. We are confronted with choices every day. These are choices as to whom we worship and serve. This is the essence of loving God with our soul.

For example, Jesus said that we cannot serve both God and money. (Matthew 6:24) That is a daily challenge for all of us. We can worship money without even knowing it. Money can be worshiped for the security it brings. Money is status. Money is power. Money buys things; it equates to what I can own for myself. And money is in short supply. We compete for who has more of it.

I remember an incident when I was in my mid-twenties, before becoming a Christ follower. My wife and I went to Kmart to buy some wooden shutters for a window. They were shrink-wrapped in a package of four, but they were priced individually. When we got to the checkout, the clerk rang up all four at the price of one. I was elated; I was getting a great buy! I nudged my wife to keep quiet. I knew what was happening and I did not want the mistake exposed. When we got out to our car, my wife was overflowing with conviction, so I told her she could go back to pay for all four. She returned a few minutes later. The store officials told her it would be too difficult to reissue the purchase, so just leave the transaction as it was purchased. When I heard the "good news" I was elated all over again; I still had my good deal. But my wife was still convicted that we had not done what was right.

My wife was seeking God's kingdom and righteousness. She was worshiping God with her choices. In comparison, I was seeking the ways of this world and my fleshly desires. The devil was pleased with my choices and attitude. I may have saved twenty bucks, but I was making a choice for eternity. I was clearly pursuing the love of money over love for God. My own soul was caught between two kingdoms, and I chose the world and my flesh over the eternal kingdom of God.

I crossed over to the other side (repentance) a few years later. I became a Christ follower. And my old ways had to be reformed. I was challenged many times in those first days of choosing to follow Jesus. I would go through a checkout line, and the cashier would give me too much change. And I had to tell her, "You made a mistake. You gave me too much." Jesus was testing my new resolve. Was I going to serve God or money? The cashier was usually thankful and surprised. Most people keep the money; they, too, make a choice.

All of life is filled with choices regarding whether we serve God or the things or aspects of this physical world. We have two lives: a life in this world and a life in the spiritual world. For now, God has ordained that we exist in both realms together. We cannot escape either one. It is not a matter of whether we live as physical beings versus spiritual beings; we must live as both. *The issue is one of love; do we love and serve God with both our body and soul, or do we love and serve the things of this world.*

Jesus referred to the devil as the prince of this world that we live in. (John 12:31, 14:30, 16:11) He is actually the prince of his own kingdom here on earth. His kingdom is physical, but like all kingdoms, it has spiritual dimensions and a spiritual rule. The devil desires for us to seek his kingdom of darkness, and Jesus implores us to seek the kingdom of God. We are all on this battle field between these two kingdoms. Which side are we on? Which side do we serve? Which side do we love? Which one do we claim as our citizenship? The battles are very real, and they constitute how we live our lives and who we serve and love as Lord. Paul warned us about the spiritual attacks of the devil.

> Clothe yourselves with the full armor of God so that you may be able to stand against the schemes of the devil. For our struggle is not against flesh and blood, but against the rulers, against the powers, against the world rulers of this darkness, against the spiritual forces of evil in the heavens. Ephesians 6:11-12 (NET)

This life is a battle between two kingdoms. It is a battle fought for the souls of men and women. It is a very real battle with the most severe consequences of any battle ever fought—the outcome is eternal. The questions for all of us: Which side are we on? Which side are we fighting for? Which side do we love? We have to choose. We cannot choose both. We will live for one or the other.

Loving this World or Loving God

The life in this world is temporary and it is filled with sin, corruption, perversions, lies, anxieties and death. The life of the kingdom of God is eternal, and it is filled with love, peace, joy, righteous living, justice and truth. Death does not exist there. It is true life. It is our choice to live for one kingdom or the other while we live in this crossroad of life and death. We cannot live for both, no more than we can walk in opposing directions at the same time. Which life do we love? Which do we hate? Jesus made our choice very clear.

> The man who loves his life will lose it, while the man who hates his life in this world will keep it for eternal life. John 12:25 (NIV)

How do we love God? If we make the choice to love this world, we do not love God. In fact, if we love the world, we have chosen to hate God, to become his enemy. The world opposes God, how can we serve the world and love God at the same time?

> You adulterous people, don't you know that friendship with the world is hatred toward God? Anyone who chooses to be a friend of the world becomes an enemy of God. James 4:4 (NIV)

Our life is a combination of a physical being, our bodies, and our spiritual being, our souls. Our choice regarding how to live is a physical versus a spiritual life choice. If we chose to love the world, we do not love God.

> **Do not love this world nor the things it offers you**, for **when you love the world, you do not have the love of the Father in you**. For the world offers only a craving for physical pleasure, a craving for everything we see, and pride in our achievements and possessions. These are not from the Father, but are from this world. And this world is fading away, along with everything that people crave. But **anyone who does what pleases God will live forever**. 1 John 2:15-17 (NLT)

This is the struggle that we live in today in this world. Which life will we live for, the physical life in this world or the spiritual life in the world to come? For now, we have to live both, but which one will we love? The one we love determines the one we will pursue.

This world we live in was not initially created as perverted and corrupt; it became perverted and corrupt. Let's look at a few examples that we all witness. We already discussed the love of money versus the love of God in Chapter 1. Jesus was quite clear; we cannot love both God and money. They are opposed; we love one and hate the other. (Luke 16:13) We live in a world where every man and woman strives to survive independently of everyone else. If I am in need, my neighbor is not normally going to share his income with me. The government may extract from his income in the form of taxes, and then help me out to some degree. But for the most part, we are all on our own to make our way through this life, providing for ourselves as best as we can. Some of us have more than others and some of us have less. And this world sees personal riches as an elite status with little concern for the less fortunate. It is a competitive "dog eat dog" world. That is not the foundation of God's kingdom. God's kingdom is one that is based on love.

For the entire law is fulfilled in one statement: Love your neighbor as yourself. Galatians 5:14 (HCSB)

We have all heard this "golden rule", "Love your neighbor as yourself." Have you ever thought about what that would look like if we all fully pursued it. Just in terms of our physical needs, no one would be without basic needs of food, clothing, shelter, medical attention, transportation and basic comforts. There would be no fear of being without, because everyone would work to provide for everyone else. In comparison, in this world, everyone works to provide for themselves at the expense of everyone else. Which way do we love most? Which way do we live? That will determine whether we love God or this world. Having money is not wrong–or even being rich. But the love of money is evil, and has the power to drive our entire life away from God. How we view money and how we use it reveals who or what we love most.

For the love of money is the root of all kinds of evil. And some people, craving money, have wandered from the true faith and pierced themselves with many sorrows. 1 Timothy 6:10 (NLT)

Loving money is one example of loving the world. Let's consider another, marriage, the sexual bond of marriage and the family. Man, woman, marriage, the sexual bond and the family with children were all part of creation before the devil deceived Eve and her husband Adam. Family was created to be beautiful, wholesome, loving, enduring, encouraging and righteous. It was created to be the place where new people entered life and where they are raised by godly and loving parents to know and to serve God by the time they are adults. Marriage was to be between one man and one woman. The bond was initially to be a lifelong bond of perfect love, an open trust without any harm of any kind. But now, with the devil in charge, what has it become?

For every two marriages we have one divorce. And now many choose just to live together without a covenant of marriage. They can enjoy many of the pleasures of marriage without having to commit and dedicate themselves for life. Sex has become a commodity for any venue. Most men and women have sex outside of marriage. Sex seems to be the most exploited of God's beauties. It is used to attract men and women for the sale of any product, whether associated with sex or not—cars, beer, clothing, entertainment, sports—anything to lure our attention if attached to sex. And free sex without a marriage commitment is a part of most television programs and movies. Children are now having sex before reaching puberty. Adultery is common place within a marriage. To make it worse, 42% of the children in the United States are born out-of-wedlock. Half of our children grow up without an intact family of their biological father and mother. Sexual criminal conduct has become a plague in our nation. Rape and child sexual abuse is rampant. And now, to make matters worse, sexual relationships and marriage between two men or two women are being promoted as normal. In fact, it is considered normal to be bisexual, transsexual or any imaginable combination. And sexual exploitation with pornography and movies that center on exposing the sexual act of two people to audiences is legal, normal and an honorably acceptable industry.

Those who love this world more than God, and his kingdom and righteousness, will follow their own sexual pleasures and support and engage in these behaviors. The range of options is immense, but mostly all of us are flooded with temptations in this arena. Jesus was very clear about the levity of these temptations and the seriousness of the outcome.

"You have heard that it was said, 'You shall not commit adultery.' But I say to you that everyone who looks at a woman with lustful intent has already committed adultery with her in his heart. If your right eye causes you to sin, tear it out and throw it away. For it is better that you lose one of your members than that your whole body be thrown into hell. And if your right hand causes you to sin, cut it off and throw it away. For it is better that you lose one of your members than that your whole body go into hell. Matthew 5:27-30 (ESV)

It should be obvious from Jesus' statements that giving in to the lusts of our sinful nature and pursuing the ways and temptations of this world are in the category of making an eternal decision of where we will spend eternity. Don't misunderstand; he is not saying that we should not be tempted. Jesus was tempted in every way we are, yet he did not sin. (Hebrews 4:15) Temptation is not sin. "Lustful intent" is sin, and it has the power to corrupt our whole being, right from our heart. To love our life in this world as opposed to loving God is to give in to our temptations and even feed them. We are to oppose and struggle against sin, which is a sign that we love God's ways more than or sinful nature and the ways of the world.

The lust for sex is one addiction this world offers, but there are many more. Think of alcohol and drugs. The world cannot live without them. We tried prohibition once, but that only lasted thirteen years, from 1920 till 1933. Alcoholism was destroying lives and families. It was a plague on society. So certain groups pushed for an amendment to the U.S. Constitution prohibiting the production and sale of alcoholic beverages. But a law did not change the driving desire to consume. The demand did not change. And now that it was illegal, supply was limited. With high demand and little supply, the price went up. That promoted all sorts of illegal production and sales. As a nation, we traded a lower consumption of alcohol for massive organized crime. After thirteen years of fighting the crime, we repealed the eighteenth amendment with the twenty-third to our Constitution. Alcohol and alcoholism was back. Today we have all sorts of other mind altering drugs: marijuana, crack cocaine, heroin, many prescription drugs like Vicodin and OxyContin, methamphetamine and the list seems endless and continues to grow. And the illegal activity to provide them is also thriving and growing.

Mind altering drugs is only one addiction. There are others. Pornography, both legal and illegal, is a huge industry and has controlled and destroyed many lives and families. Gambling has been around for thousands of years. It used to be illegal in the United States, but just like drugs and alcohol, we caved into the cravings of men and the economic opportunities and pressures. Gambling used to be limited to Las Vegas, but now nearly every state has a lottery and casinos. It has just become part of our corrupted entertaining life. It is advertised as the sale of recreation and pleasure, but it is the promotion of an addiction that has the power to rob a person, leading him or her into debt and poverty and to destroying his or her life and family.

The world and the pleasures of the world are very real. We are all in a place of temptations. We are all in a place of decision. Who will we love more, God or the world?

What We Worry About

What is worry? Worry is mental and spiritual anguish over the negative uncertainties of tomorrow. Worry is an attempt of our mind to solve tomorrow's problems today. Worry is anxiety for our future. Worry is mostly over the cares of this world. Worry has the power to smother our faith and make it unfruitful. Jesus compared it to the seeds of his word being sown among thorns.

> As for what was sown among thorns, this is the one who hears the word, but **the cares of the world and the deceitfulness of riches choke the word, and it proves unfruitful**. Matthew 13:22 (ESV)

Worry does not please God. God knows that we need food, clothing and shelter, and he promises to provide for our physical needs if we will just seek his spiritual kingdom and his righteous way of living as a first priority above the pursuit of the things of this physical life and the things of this world. That is why Jesus tells us not to worry about our life in this world. God will take care of our physical needs if we will just seek his kingdom and righteousness above all else.

> Then Jesus said to his disciples, "Therefore I tell you, do not worry about your life, what you will eat, or about your body, what you will wear. For **there is more to life than food, and more to the body than clothing**. Consider the ravens: They do not sow or reap, they have no storeroom or barn, yet God feeds them. How much more valuable are you than the birds! And which of you by worrying can add an hour to his life? So if you cannot do such a very little thing as this, why do you worry about the rest? Consider how the flowers grow; they do not work or spin. Yet I tell you, not even Solomon in all his glory was clothed like one of these! And if this is how God clothes the wild grass, which is here today and tomorrow is tossed into the fire to heat the oven, how much more will he clothe you, **you people of little faith! So do not be overly concerned about what you will eat and what you will drink, and do not worry about such things**. For all the nations of the world pursue these things, and your Father knows that you need them. **Instead, pursue his kingdom, and these things will be given to you as well.**

35

"Do not be afraid, little flock, for your Father is well pleased to give you the kingdom. Sell your possessions and give to the poor. **Provide yourselves purses that do not wear out—a treasure in heaven that never decreases**, where no thief approaches and no moth destroys. **For where your treasure is, there your heart will be also**. Luke 12:22-34 (NET)

Worry identifies what is most important to us. We all need to ask ourselves, are we more worried about our state in this world than we are about our state for eternity? In about one hundred years all seven billion people who are presently alive on the face of the earth will be dead. That should put this life into perspective when compared to eternity. If we are to worry about the future, we should be most concerned about our eternal destination and state of being. Will we be in the kingdom of God, having been transformed into the likeness of Jesus by his Spirit (salvation)? Or will we be cast out of the presence of God into outer darkness where there will be the eternal torment of weeping and gnashing of teeth due to being without the love, light, unity, truth and life of God? What will be the state and place for our eternal soul? This eternal consideration will direct our present lives, and it will also determine whether we love God or not.

Notice again Jesus' words at the end of the previous passage. We are not to be afraid or worried because our loving heavenly Father is pleased to give us his kingdom. We are encouraged and implored to live this life in such a way that we store up treasures for the life to come. Where we store up treasures will bear witness to the state of our hearts. We all make this choice of seeking the treasures of this world or seeking the treasures of the kingdom of God to come.

Spiritual Versus Physical Bodies

We are a complex creation. We take for granted how wonderfully we have been made. All of life is a mystery. We see life all around us, but we sense life as being primarily physical. A blade of grass has life. Even a child perceives that it has life. A blade of grass is obviously physical, and we can describe how it works from a physical perspective. But it has life. It functions. It grows. It reproduces; it multiplies itself by making more seeds. It either lives or dies. It has a root and a blade. The root draws water and nourishment from the soil, and the blade consumes energy from the rays of the sun. The blade consumes carbon dioxide from the air, digests it and returns oxygen to the air. The grass is made up of thousands of living cells that all work together in marvelous ways with varying functions, which unite as a living blade of grass. The grass does not have a brain. It does not think. Yet it thrives and reproduces with life all on its own. It is a miracle of life! Life in itself—without thinking or emotions or feelings—is a spiritual reality. Yes, even a blade of grass has a physical and spiritual living reality.

We have already discussed our human existence as being both physical and spiritual. We easily perceive our physical bodies. Most of us cannot fathom life without having a physical reality. But most do not perceive that without the spiritual life, the physical life is impossible. In fact, those who ignorantly and foolishly believe in evolution deny any spiritual component to life. They think that life can exist purely in the physical realm. They do not even believe in a spiritual realm. Ironically, the fact that they can even think and debate the issue reveals that we all have a spiritual life. Thinking is all spiritual. It has no physical attributes. In addition, we all have emotions and motives that are equally nonphysical. But these fools deny anything spiritual because to deny a spiritual life is necessary to deny the existence of God, who is a spiritual living being. (John 4:24)

The truth of the matter is that all things are of God who is spirit. The physical realm is a subset of the spiritual realm. The physical would not exist if not proceeding from the encompassing spiritual realm where God lives and reigns. We are bound by the physical. When Jesus returns, we will all be released from the constraints and limitations of our physical existence. Consider Paul's description of this transformation.

So is it with the resurrection of the dead. What is sown is perishable; what is raised is imperishable. It is sown in dishonor; it is raised in glory. It is sown in weakness; it is raised in power. **It is sown a natural body; it is raised a spiritual body. If there is a natural body, there is also a spiritual body.** Thus it is written, "The first man Adam became a living being"; the last Adam became a life-giving spirit. But it is not the spiritual that is first but the natural, and then the spiritual. The first man was from the earth, a man of dust; the second man is from heaven. As was the man of dust, so also are those who are of the dust, and as is the man of heaven, so also are those who are of heaven. Just as we have borne the image of the man of dust, we shall also bear the image of the man of heaven.

I tell you this, brothers: **flesh and blood cannot inherit the kingdom of God, nor does the perishable inherit the imperishable.** Behold! I tell you a mystery. We shall not all sleep, but we shall all be changed, in a moment, in the twinkling of an eye, at the last trumpet. For the trumpet will sound, and the dead will be raised imperishable, and we shall be changed. For this perishable body must put on the imperishable, and this mortal body must put on immortality. 1 Corinthians 15:42-53 (ESV)

So when Jesus proclaims that we are to love God with our soul, he is saying that we are to live for him and to seek our eternal life in his kingdom, which is filled with his spiritual life. We are not to cling to and worship our earthly, worldly existence, for we have a life prepared for us that is beyond this life. It is promised for all who seek it in this life. But we will only do so if we love God.

Reflection Questions

Have you ever asked, "Who am I?" How would you answer that question?

Describe yourself in terms of your physical makeup—your looks, your strength and your physical abilities. Now describe your spiritual makeup—your personality, your mental skills, your hopes and dreams, your ambitions and goals, your motives, what drives you, your character and anything else that defines who you are as a person.

Which is easier to describe, your physical makeup or your spiritual makeup?

How do you use the combined life of your body and soul to serve and love the ways of God versus the ways of the world?

Which kingdom do you proclaim citizenship, the kingdom of this world (darkness) or the kingdom of God (light)? (Colossians 1:10-14) What is the evidence of your citizenship?

Chapter 4

With All Your Heart

Every man and woman has a heart that resides deep within the soul. Our soul is our entire spiritual being. Our soul is made up of several components, the heart, spirit and mind. It is similar to our physical bodies that are an assembly of many components into one functional living body—legs, arms, head, all of our internal organs and more. They all miraculously function together as one living being. Our body is our entire physical life. Could the body live without the heart or the lungs or the stomach or the liver? We need all of the parts working together to make up a living being. The same is true for our living spiritual being, the living soul.

So let's take a look at a few of the parts that make up the soul. What is the difference between our spirit and our heart? A clear biblical definition of each does not exist, but we do have several verses that provide some understanding. Our heart is the place where our spirit(s) resides. After Jesus was resurrected, he sent back his Spirit to reside within us. So where does the Spirit reside? In our hearts.

He anointed us, set his seal of ownership on us, and **put his Spirit in our hearts** as a deposit, guaranteeing what is to come. 2 Corinthians 1:21-22 (NIV)

And because you are sons, God has sent the **Spirit of His Son into our hearts**, crying, "*Abba*, Father!" Galatians 4:6 (HCSB)

We have physical hearts that pump blood around in our body, and we have spiritual hearts. They are not the same, but it is not a coincidence that in the Bible they have the same name. This is not just an English translational coincidence. The Hebrew word for the spiritual heart and the physical heart also uses the same word: "labe". This same Hebrew word is used to refer to God's heart. Remember, we were created in the image of God. We have a heart like God's.

Heart is used numerous times in the New Testament using the Greek word, "kardia"; referring to the spiritual heart. However, there are no occurrences of the physical heart in the New Testament for comparison of the spiritual and the physical use of the word. It is curious, though, that we use the English word, cardiac, referring to our physical heart, which is similar to the Greek "kardia", which references our spiritual heart in the New Testament.

Our human hearts are essential for bodily human life. The heart pumps blood to provide the essential nutrients of life throughout the body that provide the energy for functional life. The blood supplies oxygen to every living cell. It also removes all of the waste products and contaminants. The blood is also the substance that carries all of the antibodies that fight off infectious germs and even cancerous cells. Blood transports hormones, which are chemical messengers that regulate the function of every living cell of the body. The heart pumps the blood that permeates the life of every cell of the body. Every cell depends upon the heart and blood for its life.

When the heart stops, life stops. If the heart is weak or malfunctions, the body is weak and malfunctions. The Bible states that the life of the body is in the blood. (Leviticus 17:10-14, Deuteronomy 12:23) Jesus gave up his life for us by shedding his blood. (1 Corinthians 10:16, Ephesians 2:13, Hebrew 9:14, 1 Peter 1:18-19)

We all have a physical heart that provides the life of the body, but we all have a spiritual heart that provides the life of our soul. This spiritual heart is the wellspring of life, or it can be a dungeon of death.

Guard your heart above all else, for it is the source of life. Proverbs 4:23 (HCSB)

See to it, brothers and sisters, that none of you has an **evil, unbelieving heart that forsakes the living God**. Hebrews 3:12 (NET)

Hearts that Cannot Love

We have a dilemma; we are commanded to love God and others from our hearts, but we were born into this world with selfish, evil hearts. How are we to love if we are not able? We are commanded to love God with all of our heart, but we were born with hearts that were incapable of loving God with ALL of our hearts. It's even worse. We can be deceived into thinking that our hearts are okay. We don't see the evil that lurks within them. We are unaware of the vile fruit that comes forth from our corrupted hearts.

The human heart is the most deceitful of all things, and desperately wicked. Who really knows how bad it is? But I, the LORD, search all hearts and examine secret motives. I give all people their due rewards, according to what their actions deserve." Jeremiah 17:9-10 (NLT)

I was raised in a church-going family. I went to church, Sunday school, and even went to a Christian school from sixth to eighth grades. But in spite of being subjected to many church teachings, my relationship with God was nearly non-existent. Looking back, my heart was more dedicated to pursuing pleasures of many kinds. Pleasure is not necessarily wrong, but it can come before God. And in my case, many of my pursuits were wrong. I craved wild living. I loved to have sinful, destructive and wild fun. While proclaiming to be a Christian, my mouth flowed with vulgarities, which included taking God's name in vain—using his name to make a disgusting emphasis about anything. My heart was set on sexual fulfillment with women and pornography and lust. To make it all worse, I bragged about my sinful pursuits. And worse yet, I could not see myself. I did not see my sinful heart. I was unaware of how I aroused God's jealousy. My heart was corrupt and dead to the life of God. And I did all this while professing to be a Christian. I had no idea of what it truly meant to be a Christ-follower.

Jesus fully understands the wicked state of the human heart. It may be difficult to see within our hearts, but we can easily see all of the evil that is clearly evident in the world around us. Our own lives contribute to the fallen state of the world in which we strive to find life. Our mouths can be filled with perverse and damaging words. And all this comes from the evil within our own hearts. These are the hearts from which we are to love God. Jesus clearly pinpointed the source of our evil.

> But the words you speak come **from the heart**—that's what defiles you. For **from the heart** come evil thoughts, murder, adultery, all sexual immorality, theft, lying, and slander. Matthew 15:18-19 (NLT)

What a dilemma! How can we possibly love God with hearts like that? Now what do we do? Well, "with God all things are possible." (Matthew 19:26) We talk a lot about being saved, but do we really know what we have been saved from? *Eternal life is the outcome of our relationship with God. In other words, God is life, and we receive the flow of his life through our relationship with him. This life manifests from a relationship with God Almighty—he loves me and I love him. Without his love for me, there is no relationship. And without my love for him, there is no relationship.*

Granted, first he has loved me in all of my depravity. But then God has provided a means for me to love him. It is all God's doing, but make no mistake in understanding; without my love for him, his life does not occur in me. *In his love for me, he has provided a means for me to love him, and he does this by giving me his Spirit so that I can have a new heart that is capable of loving him.*

> I will sprinkle you with pure water and you will be clean from all your impurities. I will purify you from all your idols. **I will give you a new heart**, and **I will put a new spirit within you**. I will remove the heart of

stone from your body and give you a heart of flesh. **I will put my Spirit within you; I will take the initiative and you will obey my statutes and carefully observe my regulations.** Ezekiel 36:25-27 (NET) [See also Ezekiel 11:19-21]

Notice that love for God is not a matter of professing good, warm feelings about God. Love for God is seen in our heartfelt desire to obey the statues and regulations of God. Our love for God is revealed in how we live for him. Enoch was a righteous man with a heart for God. He walked with God and pleased God. Enoch never died; God just took him up to himself. (Genesis 5:24, Hebrews 11:5)

In the garden, before Adam and Eve disobeyed God's command, they enjoyed the life that proceeded from God. The Bible says that they walked with God. God provided all that they needed for all of life. It was perfect, and it overflowed with the beauty and pleasantries of God's life. When the Bible says that they walked with God, it means that they lived their lives in harmony with the one who created them and who breathed into them the breath of life. As long as they obediently remained harmonious with God, their beautiful life would continue to flow—forever—eternally.

The garden was abundant in fruit trees of which they could reach out and eat and enjoy. But there was one tree in the middle of the garden that was not to be eaten from, the tree of the knowledge of good and evil. Clearly, this was not a normal fruit tree as we know it. Many describe the fruit as an apple, which misses the importance of this forbidden tree. Its fruit was "the knowledge of good and evil". Imagine Adam and Eve's existence. They had never witnessed evil of any kind. Their relationships with God and with one another were perfect. Sin was nonexistent. Their understanding was total innocence. The concept of good versus evil was completely foreign to them. Their trust in each other and in God was perfect. They had no fear of any kind. Their love was perfect. There was no shame of any sort. They were totally naked before each other and God. And this nakedness was more than physical. They had no need to hide anything of their hearts or minds from each other. They were perfectly innocent—not knowing good versus evil.

God warned them not to eat of this forbidden tree of the knowledge of good and evil because it would contaminate their perfect relationship and the result would be death. But they were tempted. They disobeyed God and they ate of it. There were several aspects of the temptation, but the overriding temptation was one of independence of God. All of their blessings, all provision and even their life came from God. The serpent convinced Eve that if she ate of this forbidden tree that she would be like God, knowing good and evil. She would have God's wisdom. And the tree was filled with pleasantries. Eve was tempted with the thought of what it would be like to go out on her own, in her own will, and without a need to submit or depend upon God for life. She believed the lie, and so do most of her offspring.

Now they were no longer innocent, and all of their offspring were not innocent, which includes us at this present time. They now knew good versus evil first hand; their perfect innocence was gone forever. In fact, evil increasingly pervades every aspect of life. And just as the serpent deceived Eve, he deceives us. The world craves evil. And just as Eve believed the deceiver, so we have believed him. The devil convinced Eve that God was lying to her. He convinced her that she would not die if she ate of the forbidden tree; rather he tempted her with the thought that she would become wise—like God. And, in addition, the fruit was filled with pleasure.

Eve had a choice to make. Would she obey God or the devil? Would she turn away from God in order to follow her own desires, or would she remain loyally committed to the one who loved her? Would she believe the serpent or believe God? She had to choose which one was lying to her. She chose to believe the serpent, which meant that God was the liar in her mind.

Love is a choice. And without choice, we cannot love. Obedience is a choice, and so is disobedience. That is why God said that he would give us a new heart by giving to us his Spirit. And why? To move us to obey his commands. To love God is to obey his commands. Life proceeds from God by living our lives according to his commands, his ways of living. All else is darkness and death. *This is the essence of being saved, to be brought back into an obedient relationship with God so that we will have his life again.* That is why Jesus came, to restore this love relationship with God, which is a decision on our part—from our hearts—to follow God's decrees. It is a love for these decrees, for from them we find life.

How blessed is the one who does not follow the advice of the wicked, or stand in the pathway with sinners, or sit in the assembly of scoffers! Instead **he finds pleasure in obeying the LORD's commands; he meditates on his commands day and night.** He is like a tree planted by flowing streams; it yields its fruit at the proper time, and its leaves never fall off. He succeeds in everything he attempts. Not so with the wicked! Instead they are like wind-driven chaff. **For this reason the wicked cannot withstand judgment, nor can sinners join the assembly of the godly. Certainly the LORD guards the way of the godly, but the way of the wicked ends in destruction.** Psalm 1:1-6 (NET)

We all want eternal life, but what does that mean? What does that entail? God warned Adam and Eve about death. He warned them not to eat of the forbidden tree so that they would not die. But they did not believe him. We are faced with the same choice. It is a choice to know and believe that true life is dependent upon living according to God's ways of living. God's precepts, his statues, his laws—these were all given to guide men into life by following them. To love God is not to obey him out of guilt or out of the fear of retribution. We obey out of the love for his commands, for in them we find life—his life—eternal life.

I will never forget your precepts, for by them you have preserved my life. Psalm 119:93 (NIV)

Trouble and distress have come upon me, but your commands are my delight. **Your statutes are forever right; give me understanding that I may live.** Psalm 119:143-144 (NIV)

Your compassion is great, O LORD; **preserve my life according to your laws.** Psalm 119:156 (NIV)

To love God with all of our hearts is to seek out God's ways of living so that we can walk in them and find life—eternal life. We do not seek to obey his commands out of the fear of punishment or to somehow make ourselves good. We seek his commands out of the love for his commands from the motivations of our hearts. This is loving God with our hearts.

Blessed are they whose ways are blameless, who walk according to the law of the LORD. Blessed are they who keep his statutes and seek him with all their heart. They do nothing wrong; they walk in his ways. You have laid down precepts that are to be fully obeyed. Psalm 119:1-4 (NIV)

How can a young man keep his way pure? By living according to your word. **I seek you with all my heart; do not let me stray from your commands.** I have hidden your word in my heart that I might not sin against you. Praise be to you, O LORD; teach me your decrees. Psalm 119:9-12 (NIV)

Jesus has given us his own Spirit to reside within our hearts and so become a wellspring of life within us. It is like a flowing well of "living water". Without his Spirit, we are powerless to love. We are like a dried up well. But with his Spirit, we have an ever-flowing source of the living water of God.

Jesus talked about this living water with a Samaritan woman as she was about to draw water from a well.

Jesus answered her, "If you knew the gift of God and who it is that asks you for a drink, you would have asked him and he would have given you **living water**."

"Sir," the woman said, "you have nothing to draw with and the well is deep. Where can you get this **living water**? Are you greater than our father Jacob, who gave us the well and drank from it himself, as did also his sons and his flocks and herds?"

Jesus answered, "Everyone who drinks this water will be thirsty again, but **whoever drinks the water I give him will never thirst. Indeed, the water I give him will become in him a spring of water welling up to eternal life**."

The woman said to him, "Sir, give me this water so that I won't get thirsty and have to keep coming here to draw water." John 4:10-15 (NIV)

We think of a desert as a dry and sandy plain with no life. For the most part, nothing grows there. So, what makes a desert? How did it get there? It is arid; there is no rain. Life does not exist without water. That is why scientists look for water on other planets to see if it could possibly sustain life. If rain were to suddenly fall upon a desert, in a short time we would witness life coming up from the ground. And other life forms would inhabit the land. The opposite is also true. Imagine a lush green land that is filled with vegetation of all kinds—trees, grass, flowers, vegetables, fruit and the like. Now remove the water; bring forth a drought. All vegetation will die within one season. If the drought remains, the land will become a barren desert wasteland. The same is true for each one of us without the wellspring of life, the Spirit of the living God. Without this well-spring of life living within us, we become a dried up desert inside.

Yes, God, in his grace and mercy, has provided a means for us to have his life abounding within our own hearts. And from these living hearts we are capable of loving God and loving others. Without his Spirit, we are nothing more than a fruitless wasteland.

The Devil's Same Lie Still Works

Eve was ignorant of the devil's schemes due to her innocence. She had never before seen evil or sin or even lies. She had never been responsible for understanding good versus evil. But this is not so for us. We live in a world that is consumed by evil. Does that make us wiser?

People refer to being street smart. By this they mean that we need to be aware of what goes on among the evil people who live in dark places, for they are out to take advantage of us. So does that mean that the ones who live in the streets are wise? No! If they were wise, they would flee the streets where evil thrives.

It is not just street people who need wisdom. They are not the only ones who have been deceived. The devil uses the same lie that he gave to Eve. He convinced her that disobedience would not result in death. He deceives us in like manner.

Obedience has been portrayed by the world as restrictive and lifeless. Many places within the Church have even been portrayed obedience as legalistic and unnecessary. The blood of Jesus has been portrayed as being shed so that we can continue in disobedience without consequence. It is as though we can gain the blessings of God without having an intimate relationship of obedience to him. It has become a license of rebellion. The grace of God has become a license for immorality.

I say this because some ungodly people have wormed their way into your churches, **saying that God's marvelous grace allows us to live immoral lives.** The condemnation of such people was recorded long ago, for they have denied our only Master and Lord, Jesus Christ. Jude 1:4 (NLT)

I left a church once because both pastors were adamant that we did not need to turn from our sinful ways. They contended that since Jesus' death on the cross, we no longer needed to repent of our sins. They said, "We are saved by faith, not by works." They saw turning from our sinful ways as a work of the flesh. When I told them of my past life of sin and how the Spirit of God and the word of God changed me so that I no longer participated in many of my past sinful practices, the senior pastor said, "Oh Gary; you don't believe that do you?"

They had no understanding of the destructive nature of sin and how Jesus came to bring life, to turn us away from wallowing in death by our evil practices.

A few weeks prior to leaving I was in the midst of ten to fifteen members of this church. A question came up that floored me: "Will there be sin in heaven?" No one knew the answer. Their logic went like this: "If our sin is forgiven here on earth by the blood of Jesus, wouldn't our sin in heaven also be forgiven?" These people had been led astray, and they had no understanding of the deathly nature of sin. Jesus came to deliver us from the sin that is robbing all of us of his life. He came to free us by his Spirit so that we can truly live and have his life within us, among us and in all that we think, do and say.

This world speaks the same lie. The devil is ruler over this world. He told Eve that she would not truly die if she disobeyed God. He tells us the same lie today in various forms. Freedom has become the new morality. It says that true life is born in the freedom to live life any way that we desire for our self. We decide what is right or wrong, good or bad. Freedom to set our own standards is what brings forth life for us. And what is good and best for you is decided by you. Who are we to judge? Tolerance is life, not obedience. Obedience has been construed as narrow-minded. And this new tolerance is portrayed as true love for others, and to judge right and wrong is unloving. This new theology portrays Jesus as the one who gave his life so that we could live the way we please without judgment, punishment or the wrath of God. And this is all portrayed as God's love for us. This deceptive theology implies that God loved us so much that he now gives us the freedom to live any way we decide, and all will be freely forgiven without consequence. It also implies that our love for God is based on the joy of this new freedom we have to go our own way that was paid for by the blood of Jesus. "What a wonderful God who doesn't judge or condemn or punish anymore". This thinking is a mockery of God's will and the tremendous sacrifice that he made to restore a true relationship with him. The writer of Hebrews clearly warns us against such an evil deception.

If we deliberately keep on sinning after we have received the knowledge of the truth, no sacrifice for sins is left, but only a fearful expectation of judgment and of raging fire that will consume the enemies of God. Anyone who rejected the law of Moses died without mercy on the testimony of two or three witnesses. How much more severely do you think a man deserves to be punished who has trampled the Son of God under foot, who has treated as an unholy thing the blood of the covenant that sanctified him, and who has insulted the Spirit of grace? For we know him who said, "It is mine to avenge; I will repay," and again, "The Lord will judge his people." It is a dreadful thing to fall into the hands of the living God. Hebrews 10:26-31 (NIV)

God desires a marriage relationship with us. He desires to give us his heart by his Spirit, and he desires to have ours as evidenced by giving our lives to him. It is not love for God if we proclaim the blood of Jesus and then to selfishly go about our lives as though God is not part of them. If God is not our first priority—from our hearts—then we are not walking in unity with him as our God, as our husband, and not even as our Savior. *Christianity and salvation are all about restoring an intimate relationship with God our Father. Without obedience to God, there is no relationship.*

God is life; there is no other. There is no other source of life. This life is poured into us through an obedient and intimate relationship with God. Jesus came so that we could and would drink from him the water of life.

But whoever drinks some of the water that I will give him will never be thirsty again, but the water that I will give him **will become in him a fountain of water springing up to eternal life**." John 4:14 (NET)

Notice that we obtain eternal life by drinking this water of life. This is not about believing special doctrines of truth, as important as knowing and believing truth may be. This is about living out the truth. This is about seeking the one who is truth, namely Jesus. This is about living for him and following him. This is not about legalism—being under the written law. This is about having the law of the Spirit living within us. It is about having a new heart of the Spirit residing within us as Ezekiel prophesized. (Ezekiel 36:25-27 given in the previous chapter) With this new heart we are compelled to live in the new way of the Spirit of God. And in this new way, our relationship with God is restored. By the Spirit that he puts into our hearts, we now belong to him. Notice in the follow words of Paul the emphasis he puts on our relationship with God, and that this relationship is one of belonging to God. We are his possession. Before this, our sinful nature was hostile to our relationship with him and could not please him. But now that we belong to him by being born again of his Spirit, we desire to please him. Our heart-to-heart relationship has been restored.

So now there is no condemnation for those **who belong to Christ Jesus**. And **because you belong to him**, the power of the life-giving Spirit has freed you from the power of sin that leads to death. The law of Moses was unable to save us because of the weakness of our sinful nature. So God did what the law could not do. He sent his own Son in a body like the bodies we sinners have. And in that body **God declared an end to sin's control over us** by giving his Son as a sacrifice for our sins. He did this so that the just requirement of the law would be fully satisfied for us, **who no longer follow our sinful nature but instead follow the Spirit.**

Those who are dominated by the sinful nature think about sinful things, but **those who are controlled by the Holy Spirit think about things that please the Spirit**. So **letting your sinful nature control your mind leads to death. But letting the Spirit control your mind leads to life and peace.** For the **sinful nature is always hostile to God**. It never did obey God's laws, and it never will. That's why those who are still under the control of their sinful nature **can never please God.**

But you are not controlled by your sinful nature. You are controlled by the Spirit if you have the Spirit of God living in you. (**And remember that those who do not have the Spirit of Christ living in them do not belong to him at all.**) Romans 8:1-9 (NLT)

Paul is describing the fulfillment of Ezekiel's prophesy more than 600 years before the Spirit was actually poured out on those who are in Christ Jesus.

I will give you a new heart and put a new spirit in you; I will remove from you your heart of stone and give you a heart of flesh. And **I will put my Spirit in you and move you to follow my decrees and be careful to keep my laws.** Ezekiel 36:26-27 (NIV)

The Spirit of God was given to us so that we would have living hearts that would be capable of loving God in obedience to the law of the Spirit of life, rather than the written law. By God's grace, we now have the power to love God, to please him and to acquire his life. We now have the Spirit's power to deny the temptations of the sinful nature and to live according to the life of the Spirit within us.

So I say, live by the Spirit, and you will not gratify the desires of the sinful nature. For the sinful nature desires what is contrary to the Spirit, and the Spirit what is contrary to the sinful nature. They are in conflict with each other, so that you do not do what you want. **But if you are led by the Spirit, you are not under law.** Galatians 5:16-18 (NIV)

God has purchased us with the blood of Christ. He has redeemed us from the world, from the hand of Satan, yes, even from ourselves—that is, our sinful nature. We belong to him now, as a bride belongs to her husband. He paid the price to have a singular relationship such that he does not share our affection for him with anyone or anything else.

Don't you realize that your body is the temple of the Holy Spirit, who lives in you and was given to you by God? **You do not belong to yourself, for God bought you with a high price.** So you must honor God with your body. 1 Corinthians 6:19-20 (NLT)

This understanding is foundational for loving God. For without the living Spirit of God giving his life to our own hearts, we are powerless to love God and obey his commands. Without his Spirit, we are powerless to please him.

Jesus came and died for our sins so that our sins would be forgiven,
So that *our relationship with God would be reconciled,*
So that *God would send his Spirit to live within us,*
So that *we would have the power to live as Christ,*
So that *we would love God and live for him,*
So that *we would be a kingdom of priest, reigning with Jesus.*
So that *together we would have eternal life.*

*If we stop after the first "**so that**", we miss the power and purposes of God completely. And loving God with our hearts becomes impossible without a new heart from God by his Spirit.*

Jesus told the woman at the well that he would give her a spring of living water that would well up in her to give her eternal life. This is the free gift of God for us. We now have access to life itself. This flow of life can live within our own hearts. But we must understand what a precious and powerful gift we have been given and we must protect it. For if we ignore it, and if we continue to sow to the sinful nature, we will not take hold of this gift of life that was freely given to us.

Above all else, guard your heart, for it is the wellspring of life. Proverbs 4:23 (NIV)

We are called to take hold of this life that is truly life. It has been freely given to us, but we must take hold of it.

In this way they will lay up treasure for themselves as a firm foundation for the coming age, so that they may **take hold of the life that is truly life**. 1 Timothy 6:19 (NIV)

Reflection Questions

Have you been born again of the Spirit of God? What is the evidence based on your new life? Do you have a new heart of the Spirit living within you? How do you know?

How has his Spirit changed your relationship with God?

How do you make God jealous? In other words, what things of your life come before your love for God?

Chapter 5

Overcoming a Hardened Heart

As already discussed, without the Spirit of God residing within our individual hearts, we are just dried up wells with no provision of life. We are dead inside without the capability of loving God with all of our hearts. His Spirit gives us the wisdom to know God's own heart and mind. (1 Corinthians 2:6-16) But it would be naïve to think that now that we have his Spirit that we will just automatically do what is right and love God as he desires. We have been given his Spirit, but we must also sow to his Spirit. So, what does this mean? What does it entail?

We were all born with a nature that drove the motivations of our hearts prior to receiving his Spirit that now lives within the hearts of God's chosen children. The Bible calls this old nature our sinful nature or the nature of the flesh. It is a nature that is self-seeking. It seeks self-gratification and pleasure. It is prone to selfishness and pride. It is the birthplace of sin. It opposes the nature of the Spirit. The sinful nature and the Spirit within us each have the ability lead our motivations, thinking and behaviors, but in opposite directions.

Being born again by the Spirit gives us a new life in Jesus Christ with a new nature. But that does not automatically mean that the old nature, the sinful nature, has lost its power and desire to rule our lives. It's quite the contrary. There is a battle between the two natures. They both desire to have control of us. However, the Spirit of God within us is more powerful than the sinful nature, and it has the ability to put to death the deeds of the sinful nature.

Caution: Just having the Holy Spirit within us does not mean that we will automatically crucify the sinful nature. It is always our choice to do so. We must choose to die to self and live for Christ in every situation. We are commanded to love God with all of our heart. Loving God is a choice we make. And when we deny the desires of our flesh, our sinful nature, and choose to live by the motivations of the Spirit within us, we are also choosing to love God with our hearts. Love is always a choice. To love is to give up some aspect of our lives for the benefit of someone else. To love God with our hearts is to give up the desires of our flesh so that the desires of the Spirit can be met in our lives—for the glory of God.

Let's look at some passages to reveal this conflict. Paul wrote to the Galatians about these two forces at work within us that are vying for who will reign in our lives. It is our choice as to which one will rule.

You, my brothers, were called to be free. But **do not use your freedom to indulge the sinful nature**; rather, serve one another in love. The entire law is summed up in a single command: "Love your neighbor as yourself." If you keep on biting and devouring each other, watch out or you will be destroyed by each other.

So I say, **live by the Spirit, and you will not gratify the desires of the sinful nature. For the sinful nature desires what is contrary to the Spirit, and the Spirit what is contrary to the sinful nature. They are in conflict with each other, so that you do not do what you want**. But if you are led by the Spirit, you are not under law.

The **acts of the sinful nature** are obvious: sexual immorality, impurity and debauchery; idolatry and witchcraft; hatred, discord, jealousy, fits of rage, selfish ambition, dissensions, factions and envy; drunkenness, orgies, and the like. I warn you, as I did before, that those who live like this will not inherit the kingdom of God.

But the **fruit of the Spirit** is love, joy, peace, patience, kindness, goodness, faithfulness, gentleness and self-control. Against such things there is no law. **Those who belong to Christ Jesus have crucified the sinful nature with its passions and desires**. Since we live by the Spirit, let us keep in step with the Spirit. Let us not become conceited, provoking and envying each other. Galatians 5:13-26 (NIV)

Here is the conflict that resides within us: Do we live to satisfy the desires and cravings of our own sinful nature, or do we live to bring pleasure and glory to the Spirit God has given us? Will we sow to death or to life. Will we choose to love God more than our fleshly nature and the things of this world?

Don't be misled—you cannot mock the justice of God. You will always harvest what you plant. Those who live only to **satisfy their own sinful nature** will harvest decay and death from that sinful nature. But **those who live to please the Spirit** will harvest everlasting life from the Spirit. So let's not get tired of doing what is good. At just the right time we will reap a harvest of blessing if we don't give up. Therefore, whenever we have the opportunity, we should do good to everyone—especially to those in the family of faith. Galatians 6:7-10 (NLT)

When we are born again of the Spirit of God we become children of God. That is the meaning of being born again. We were once born to our earthly fathers, but now we are born to our heavenly Father by receiving the new nature of his Spirit living within our hearts. As his children, we have an obligation to live for him by his Spirit within us, and not to live for the sinful nature that still resides, as evident in the fact that we are still physical human beings. In other words, we are to live for the life of our spiritual being over our fleshly being.

So then, brothers and sisters, we are under obligation, not to the flesh, to live according to the flesh (for if you live according to the flesh, you will die), but **if by the Spirit you put to death the deeds of the body**

you will live. For **all who are led by the Spirit of God are the sons of God**. Romans 8:12-14 (NET)

Hardening Our Heart

We have already referred to the promise in Ezekiel that God would take out our hearts of stone and give us hearts of flesh by giving us his Spirit.

And I will give you a new heart, and I will put a new spirit in you. I will take out your **stony, stubborn heart** and give you a **tender, responsive heart.** Ezekiel 36:26 (NLT)

In spite of receiving this new heart, we are fully capable of returning to our hard heart of stone that is stubborn, disobedient and unbelieving of God. It would be easy to live for God in all circumstances if there were no trials to face. But this life is filled with trials that test our faith and resolve. When hardship and suffering come into our lives, what will we do? Whom will we serve now? And will our faith and belief in God carry us through? Or will pain, distrust and fear overwhelm us?

Consider it pure joy, my brothers, whenever you face trials of many kinds, because you know that the testing of your faith develops perseverance. Perseverance must finish its work so that you may be mature and complete, not lacking anything. James 1:2-4 (NIV)

Notice that it says "the testing of our faith". Our faith is not tested without a trial, a struggle of life. These are the places where we can go in either direction. We can remain faithful to God and give him glory, or we can complain and question God's goodness and love for us. To love God with our hearts is to remain faithful to God's promises, continuing to put our hope in him no matter what the circumstances. And this means that we will do what is right according to the Spirit and not give in to our fleshly desires—even in the midst of a trial. Our love for God is proved genuine when under trials, not when everything is going well.

We have a perfect example of stubborn, hard hearts from the episode of God's people when they were delivered from over four hundred years of slavery in Egypt. He delivered them with ten miraculous plagues and the parting of the Red Sea. They were elated in worship at the time. But then God led them out into the desert. This was the journey to the land of promise. And even in their desert crossing he provided shade from the sun by day and a fire to keep them warm at night. He caused water to flow from a rock in the desert. And he rained down manna from heaven for food each day. With all these miracles of deliverance, protection and provision one would think that they would remain thankful and obedient as they rested in God for their future. But that was not the case. They complained and rebelled the entire way. (Begin reading at Exodus 15:22 for the account.)

The book of Hebrews warns us not to harden our hearts as the Israelites did in the desert. In fact, the Holy Spirit warns us.

Therefore, as the Holy Spirit says,

"Today, if you hear his voice, **do not harden your hearts** as in the rebellion, on the day of testing in the wilderness, where your fathers put me to the test and saw my works for forty years. Therefore I was provoked with that generation, and said, 'They **always go astray in their heart**; they have not known my ways.' As I swore in my wrath, 'They shall not enter my rest.' "

Take care, brothers, lest there be in any of you an evil, unbelieving heart, leading you to fall away from the living God. But exhort one another every day, as long as it is called "today," that none of you may be hardened by the deceitfulness of sin. For we have come to share in Christ, if indeed we hold our original confidence firm to the end. As it is said,

"**Today, if you hear his voice, do not harden your hearts** as in the rebellion."

For who were those who heard and yet rebelled? Was it not all those who left Egypt led by Moses? And with whom was he provoked for forty years? Was it not with those who sinned, whose bodies fell in the wilderness? And to whom did he swear that they would not enter his rest, but to those who were disobedient? So we see that they were unable to enter because of unbelief. Hebrews 3:7-19 (ESV)

Grumbling and complaining is a sign that our hearts are becoming hard. The Israelites began their complaining just three weeks after being delivered from their bondage in Egypt, and they never stopped complaining. (Exodus 15:24, 162, 7-9, 12, 17:3, Numbers 14:2, 27-29, 36, 16:11, 41, 17:5, 10, Deuteronomy 1:27)

How often do we grumble and complain about our lives—the lives God has ordained for us? How often do we humbly thank God for all that he has provided and done for us? How often do we thank him for his wonderful promises for us? Remember, the Israelites complained as they were on their journey to the Promised Land. We are on a similar journey. We are promised to inherit eternal life and the kingdom of God. (James 2:5, Matthew 19:29) So, do we complain about this life as we wait for these promises to be fulfilled? Through Jesus we have already received the promised Holy Spirit as a deposit, guaranteeing what is to come. (1 Corinthians 1:22, 5:5) So do we walk in the ways of the Spirit now, or do we harden our hearts because of the hardships or trials of this life. If we are going to love God with all of our hearts, we must live with willing, tender hearts toward his will and the ways of his Spirit, whom he has freely given us.

Let's consider a few examples. What about marriage and divorce? We have about one divorce for every two marriages in a given year. And these figures are true for those who claim to be Christ followers. God hates divorce. (Malachi 2:16) In spite of God's love for marriage, divorce reigns. About 70% of divorce filings are initiated by wives,[2] but that doesn't mean

---

[2] Brinig, M. (2000). 'These boots are made for walking': Why most divorce filers are women. *American Law and Economics Association,* 126-169.

that husbands are not equally responsible. If husbands or wives would seek God to discover what changes are needed in our own hearts, divorce could be eliminated. Husbands and wives need to run to Jesus instead of running from each other.

Divorce is not a new thing. Moses had to deal with hard-hearted people in his day as well. The Pharisees challenged Jesus about the lawfulness of divorcing for any reason. Jesus opposed their thinking, stating that God created marriage. He made the two as one, and stated, "Therefore, what God has joined together, let not man separate". In other words, man cannot separate what God has joined as one, so don't even try to separate (divorce). Work it out!

The Pharisees didn't like this answer, so they challenged Jesus with the fact that Moses granted divorces. Look at Jesus' response.

Jesus replied, "Moses permitted you to divorce your wives **because your hearts were hard**. But it was not this way from the beginning. Matthew 19:8 (NIV)

What did he mean by "your hearts were hard"? Well, this was in the days of Moses as he led God's people in the desert for forty years. As we have already discussed, their hearts were hard against God. They did not believe that God would protect them, provide for them or lead them to a good place in life. The same was true for their marriages. All—yes, all— marriage struggles are because of sin. Sin is relational; we sin against someone. Selfishness from either spouse is sin. Unforgiveness is sin. Complaining is sin. Not loving is sin. Abuse and neglect are sin. Stubbornness and pride are sin. Jesus came for our relationship problems. And furthermore, every spouse is a sinner—husband or wife. If you are contemplating divorce because your spouse is a sinner, consider your own sin. Jesus came so that we could forgive, so that we could overcome sin, so that we could love others—sinners. Instead of running from each other, we should be running to Jesus, the author and perfecter of our faith. (Hebrews 12:1-3)

To love God with our hearts is to trust him with our life. It is to trust him with our marriage. It is to trust him with our spouse and our self. He will work in us to will and to act according to his pleasure and purpose. He gave us his Holy Spirit to reside within us for the purpose of changing our hearts and minds. Hard hearts do not fear God. They are not thankful and they do not consider how God sees their lives. The hardhearted do not know the power of God, nor do they submit to his power. Hard hearts are quick to blame someone else for their problems. They are full of excuses. They do not believe in the power of God and the love of God. And they do not care what God thinks compared to their own motivations.

So then, my dear friends, just as you have always obeyed, not only in my presence, but now even more in my absence, **work out your own salvation with fear and trembling. For it is God who is working in you, ⌊enabling you⌋ both to desire and to work out His good purpose.** Do everything **without grumbling and arguing,** so that you may be blameless and pure, children of God who are faultless in a crooked and perverted generation, among whom you shine like stars in the world. Philippians 2:12-15 (HCSB)

A hard heart will not submit to God. Hard hearts demand their own selfish way. Hard hearts stubbornly refuse to submit and never admit that they are wrong. Hard hearts blame others, even God. The hardhearted are incapable of loving God with all of their heart.

An example of marriage was given, which most of us can identify, but we can be hardhearted in most any situation or relationship. All of life belongs to God. Do we believe that he created everything for his good purpose? Do we believe that his ways are best? Do we believe that he loves us and will come to our aid in all circumstances if we will call upon him and wait upon him? Are we willing to give up our will for the will of God? The answer to these questions in our personal situations will determine the state of our hearts—hard or soft to God. A hard heart cannot love God!

So I tell you this, and insist on it in the Lord, that you must no longer live as the Gentiles do, in the futility of their thinking. They are **darkened in their understanding and separated from the life of God because of the ignorance that is in them due to the hardening of their hearts**. Having lost all sensitivity, they have given themselves over to sensuality so as to indulge in every kind of impurity, with a continual lust for more. Ephesians 4:17-19 (NIV)

A major sign of a hard heart is complaining. What do you complain about? Complaining with thankfulness is hypocrisy. Every time you find yourself complaining, think about the state of your heart toward God.

Softening Our Hearts

It may seem obvious that if we do not want to have a hard heart, all that we need to do is stop being stubborn, stop complaining, stop being disobedient and stop rebelling against God. As obvious as this may be, it is not that simple. That is like saying the answer to our sin is to stop sinning. Now we are back to obeying the laws—if we could just do so.

Repentance is certainly what is required, but repentance has two parts. The first is to stop doing what is wrong, and the other part is to start doing what is right. Doing just one without the other is not repentance. In fact, it is powerless hypocrisy. *Repentance is to turn from a wayward life so that you can pursue true life, the way of Jesus.*

As we have already discussed, God has provided a new heart through Jesus Christ; he has given us his Spirit. But just having his Spirit is not the change in us. The change comes by living according to the Spirit, and not according to our sinful nature. By the Spirit, we have the ability to put to death the sinful nature.

So I say, live by the Spirit, and you will not gratify the desires of the sinful nature. For the sinful nature desires what is contrary to the Spirit, and the Spirit what is contrary to the sinful nature. They are in conflict with each other, so that you do not do what you want. Galatians 5:16-17 (NIV)

Therefore, brothers, we have an obligation—but it is not to the sinful nature, to live according to it. For if you live according to the sinful nature, you will die; but if by the Spirit you put to death the misdeeds of the body, you will live, because those who are led by the Spirit of God are sons of God. Romans 8:12-14 (NIV)

The ways of the Spirit and the ways of our sinful nature are opposites. We are blessed to have the Spirit, for now we have the ability to oppose the ways of the sinful nature and to seek the ways of the Spirit. Without the Spirit, the ability to overcome does not exist. But now that we have the Spirit, we still have to overcome. We still have to sow to the Spirit and not to the old nature.

So how do we sow to a soft heart toward God? What are the opposites regarding a soft heart toward God and a hard heart? What are the attributes of a hard heart versus a soft heart? In order to sow to the Spirit rather than the sinful nature, we need to recognize the two in our daily lives so that we can make conscious choices when circumstances arise. So let's look at a few of these opposing forces in our lives.

Hard Heart	Soft Heart
Complaining	Thankfulness
Unbelief (Hebrews 3:12, 19)	Faith
Disobedience (Hebrews 3:18, 4:6, 11)	Walking by the Spirit
Ignorance (Ephesians 4:18, Hebrews 3:10)	Wisdom by Word
Sensuality (Ephesians 4:19)	Fruit of Spirit
Pride	Humility

An entire book could be written on this subject, but let's look briefly at each one of these. Complaining: The scriptures referenced earlier in chapter should be studied to get a firm understanding of our complaining nature. The Israelites had a mixture of hardships from God and many promises and miraculous blessings from God. They chose to focus on the hardships and to disregard the miraculous blessings and promises. It is imperative to recognize that this was a choice on their part. And it is a daily choice for each one of us. Our lives are filled with blessings and promises, but no one goes through life without hardships and struggles of various kinds. The choice is ours; which one will we focus on. It is the old adage: Is the glass half empty or half full? Thankfulness is the opposite of complaining. It focuses on the "half full". A soft heart meditates on how much God has blessed us and all of the good things in store for us who have faith in God's love and promises for us. Paul, for example, was joyful, content and thankful in all circumstances. He endured prison, beatings, shipwrecks, and much more. And in the midst of these circumstances he was filled with rejoicing and thankfulness. He wrote to the Philippians from prison to encourage them to be joyful in all circumstances.

> Rejoice in the Lord always. Again I say, rejoice! Let everyone see your gentleness. **The Lord is near!** Do not be anxious about anything. Instead, in every situation, through prayer and petition **with thanksgiving**, tell your requests to God. And the peace of God that surpasses all understanding **will guard your hearts** and minds in Christ Jesus. Philippians 4:4-7 (NET)

Paul is instructing us to be aware of the Lord's presence in the midst of all that we struggle through in this life. This alone is reason to rejoice. We should not allow our anxious, complaining nature to overwhelm us, but we should seek God in our struggles with the understanding that God is fully aware of our lives, fully capable of intervening and that he loves us and is accomplishing his will in and through us. If we will go to him in thankfulness for all that he has done in our lives, he will hear our petitions and will guard our hearts and our thinking. Our circumstances may or may not change, but we are promised to have the peace of God in our hearts. This is the secret to Paul's contentment. It is our secret too. A complaining heart will never find contentment, and will never find victory in life. And *a complaining heart cannot love God.*

How many of us complain about our employer, our job, our boss, our fellow workers, our working conditions, our pay—anything—and then we come home and thank God at the dinner table for how he has blessed us. In our hearts we are hypocrites. The objective for us is to be joyfully thankful in all circumstances throughout the day, week, month or year.

Be joyful always; pray continually; **give thanks in all circumstances**, for **this is God's will for you in Christ Jesus**. 1 Thessalonians 5:16-18 (NIV)

The key is for us to learn to be thankful and content in our circumstances. Contentment comes from trusting God with our lives, knowing that he loves us, that his promises are true, and that we live for him and his purposes. Complaining comes from our expectation to have our own way and to be in control of our circumstances. Complaining is an attempt to gain control. It doesn't work, but we complain anyway. Thanksgiving to God proceeds from a contented heart. Contentment depends on God's strength in life, not our own or someone else's. Again, Paul expresses his contentment in the midst of being falsely accused and sent to prison.

Not that I am speaking of being in need, for I have learned in whatever situation I am to be **content**. I know how to be brought low, and I know how to abound. **In any and every circumstance**, I have learned the secret of facing plenty and hunger, abundance and need. **I can do all things through him who strengthens me**. Philippians 4:11-13 (ESV)

Paul said that we are not to be anxious because "the Lord is near". It requires faith to know this. The Israelites saw many huge miracles with their own eyes, yet they did not believe God because they were also in the midst of hardship in the desert. Without faith in God, we are not going to trust him in the midst of our trials. Ironically, if we do not trust him, we will fail in the midst of our trials. Complaining and unbelief will never solve any problem or struggle. God is pleased when we trust him and seek him in faith. Without faith, it is impossible to please him. A soft heart is one that trusts and seeks God.

> Now without faith it is impossible to please him, for the one who approaches God must believe that he exists and that he rewards those who seek him. Hebrews 11:6 (NET)

It is not so much trusting God that he will change our lives and deliver us from whatever troubles us. Rather, it is trusting God in the midst of our circumstances. It is even to go so far as to thank God for our trials because we are developing faith and character.

> Consider it a great joy, my brothers, whenever you experience various trials, knowing that the **testing of your faith** produces endurance. But endurance must do its complete work, **so that you may be mature and complete, lacking nothing**. James 1:2-4 (HCSB)

> Not only this, but we also **rejoice in sufferings**, knowing that **suffering produces endurance, and endurance, character, and character, hope**. And hope does not disappoint, because the **love of God has been poured out in our hearts through the Holy Spirit** who was given to us. Romans 5:3-5 (NET)

Notice in this last verse that "the love of God has been poured out in our hearts by the Holy Spirit". The Spirit has been given to us so that we would have the character of God and the power of God living within us. We were all born with the sinful nature, but if we have been born again by the Spirit, we have a new nature. And by the Spirit we have the power to crucify the old complaining nature. As already said, "without faith it is impossible to please God" (Hebrews 11:6). In addition, "those controlled by the sinful nature cannot please God" (Romans 8:8).

Those controlled by the sinful nature cannot please God. You, however, are controlled not by the sinful nature but by the Spirit, if the Spirit of God lives in you. And if anyone does not have the Spirit of Christ, he does not belong to Christ. Romans 8:8-9 (NIV)

The one who sows to the Spirit within him is also sowing to a soft heart toward God and pleases God. This is a choice of obedience; obedience to the sinful nature or to the Spirit within us. And to choose to obey the Spirit requires the faith that God is Lord and that he loves us such that we can trust him with our lives. It does not mean that our outward circumstances are going to change, but rather that we will trust God in the midst of our outward circumstances. We may have to trust him with relational conflicts, with health problems, with our finances, with our failures or anything in this life that can be construed as a struggle.

This life can be very confusing. It is confusing because we do not see our circumstances from God's perspective. We do not see life and this world with a large perspective that reveals God's plan and purposes. We live in ignorance, and ignorance is darkness. God has given us his Spirit and his written word so that we would become knowledgeable with his wisdom. If we want to have soft hearts, we need to apply ourselves to acquire God's knowledge and wisdom. Having a heart for God is to love God's ways for all things. We cannot say that we love God, and then pursue the ways of this world. Jesus said that he is the way. (John 14:6) If we love God we will seek to know the Way. God has given us his word so that we may know him and know true life. To love God with a soft heart is to seek his word in order to discover a new way of living. The hard heart wants to hold onto the old ways. The new way is found in the Holy Scriptures.

But as for you, continue in what you have learned and firmly believed. You know those who taught you, and you know that from childhood you have known the **sacred Scriptures, which are able to give you wisdom for salvation through faith in Christ Jesus. All Scripture is**

inspired by God and is profitable for teaching, for rebuking, for correcting, for training in righteousness, so that the man of God may be complete, equipped for every good work. 2 Timothy 3:14-17 (HCSB)

The instruction of the LORD is perfect, renewing one's life; the testimony of the LORD is trustworthy, making the inexperienced wise. The precepts of the LORD are right, making the heart glad; the command of the LORD is radiant, making the eyes light up. Psalm 19:7-8 (HCSB)

A soft heart seeks out God's wisdom and understanding from the written word that he has provided for us so that we would know him and his will and purposes. Ignorance is not bliss, as some have stated that it is. *Ignorance brings about death and destruction and separation from God.*

It all comes down to whether we are seeking the pleasures of this life or the eternal pleasures of the Spirit. A hard heart will seek out the temporary pleasures of this world over the lasting pleasures of living a righteous life before God, seeking to do what is right and pure.

Some people do not seek God because they believe that they do not need him. They believe that they are self-sufficient. They walk in pride. A soft and pliable heart toward God is not possible if our heart is filled with pride. The prideful are living in a lie. They believe that they are much more than the reality of their true nature and capabilities. A humble man is one who lives truthfully about who he is and what he does. The proud do not please God. The humble do.

Do not love this world nor the things it offers you, for **when you love the world, you do not have the love of the Father in you**. For the world offers only a craving for physical pleasure, a craving for everything we see, and pride in our achievements and possessions. These are not from the Father, but are from this world. And this world is fading away, along with everything that people crave. But **anyone who does what pleases God will live forever**. 1 John 2:15-17 (NLT)

What is the bottom line? We have talked a lot about pleasing God. A hard heart is not concerned about pleasing God. A hard heart sets a first priority of pleasing our self. In order to love God with our heart, our first priority must be to please God.

Reflection Questions

What do you complain about? Why do you complain?

Compare your thankfulness to your complaining.

How content are you with your life? How thankful are you for the details of your life (job, finances, spouse, situations—anything that affects your welfare)?

How have you complained in the midst of a hardship in your life? How have you been thankful and optimistic in the midst of a hard struggle?

Describe your faith in God. What promises of God do you stand on regarding you attitudes, thinking and actions?

Describe how you seek God's word for wisdom, for understanding, for knowing God and his promises.

How does your pride keep you from loving God?

How do you please God from your heart?

Chapter 6

With All Our Mind

We generally think of loving someone as an outward activity. If someone is hungry, I feed him. If someone needs help, I help him. If someone needs an encouraging word, I speak to him. We do not normally think of loving someone with our mind.

Now consider your spouse. What if your spouse does everything perfectly in outward behaviors? Let's use the example of a wife, since we are the bride of Christ. Assume that she does not complain. She is responsible, sacrificing, serving and giving in every desired way. But at the same time, she never thinks about you. She never misses you. She does not care about anything you think about. In fact, she loves you out of duty, and does it almost perfectly, and all that is missing is that she takes no interest in you. You are rarely on her mind. Her mind is consumed with other loves, maybe even another lover. Maybe her mind is consumed with the thoughts of someone else, leaving no time or desire to think about you or to become like-minded with you.   Would you feel loved?   I think the answer is obvious. Love is not a duty; it is something we do that is driven by the desires of our hearts and consumes our minds.

We frequently use the phrase, "falling in love". I don't think that "falling in love" is a solid foundation for marriage, but there is something about it that is very desirable—if it would last. When these infatuated feelings occur, our minds engage, and all we can think about is the one we "love". We can talk for hours, just wanting to experience the other person.

Certainly the desire to be physically close is a driver, but a bigger driver is the desire to know each other and experience what goes on in each other's mind. During these romantic times, a couple can talk on the phone for hours, just exchanging their thoughts back and forth. The conversation can be deep or trivial; it doesn't matter. They just want to experience each other's thoughts. That is what communication is, the exchange of thoughts from one to another. It is clearly a part of any love relationship. Without the exchange of thoughts, the relationship is dry, distant and without life. Exchanging thoughts is a spiritual connection, and certainly a part of a loving relationship.

"Falling in love" may also be referred to as infatuation. It is a surface relationship. At first we only know a small portion of who our lover truly is on the inside. What we don't know, we fill in with what we want to be there. Struggles arise as we start filling in the unknown with reality. Then we discover things that we dislike. We also discover all of the areas where we are not like-minded. Now the hard work of the love affair truly begins. In the "falling in love" stage we are not confronted with all of the differences and disconnects. But now, to truly love one another, we have to work through our differences in a pursuit of becoming like-minded. This understanding is foundational for being unified with anyone, especially as Christians.

> If you have any encouragement from being united with Christ, if any comfort from his love, if any fellowship with the Spirit, if any tenderness and compassion, then make my joy complete by being **like-minded, having the same love, being one in spirit and purpose. Do nothing out of selfish ambition or vain conceit, but in humility consider others better than yourselves.** Philippians 2:1-3 (NIV)

In the infatuation stage, loving each other is easy and without sacrifice. However, this stage rarely lasts very long. Eventually, reality sets in and now the hard work of coming together to pursue the same mind, same purpose, same direction and same ambitions begins. This is a marriage, and it requires walking together. And walking together requires being in agreement on what we think about life and how to live it.

Can two people walk together without agreeing on the direction? Amos 3:3 (NLT)

Each partner will have to make some changes in how they think and the direction that they travel so that the two can live out life together with the same pursuits. This unity defines our love relationship. Feelings for each other are great; they are wonderful! It is great if they can last. But when reality sets in, the only way they can possibly continue is if the two truly become one in how they think and how they decide to live out their lives together.

Knowing God

Now let's draw a similar analogy with our love for God. Do you think God wants us to know what he thinks? Do you believe that God wants to know what we think? Does he get bored with us? Do we get bored with him? Try telling your spouse that he is a bore. What does that say about the relationship? How much love can there be? How much unity can exist? Try living with your spouse, but never communicating anything about yourself, and your spouse does the same with you. What goes on in our head and heart is held private; so assume that you do not share your heart and mind on an intimate basis. How close and united could you be?

God wants a vibrant love relationship with us. He wants to become intimate with us, and that requires an exchange of our minds—his and ours. God wants us to know him. In fact, the life that he has for us requires that we know him. He is life—eternal life—and this life is only realized by having a relationship with God where we come to know him. Jesus was very clear about this.

Now **this is eternal life**: that they **may know you, the only true God, and Jesus Christ**, whom you have sent. John 17:3 (NIV)

A love relationship is two-sided. God wants us to know him, and he wants to know us—intimately—heart to heart and mind to mind. God obviously knows all things, including what goes on in our hearts and minds. But this is not just an intellectual activity when talking about a love relationship. This is a bond of becoming like-minded. It is a bond of walking together in the same direction.

Knowing each other, being like-minded and walking together in the same direction is the substance of this love relationship with God. But what if we start this union without being like-minded? Who is going to change their mind, I or God?

To answer this, let's go back to life with God in the Garden of Eden. Adam and Eve walked with God. (Genesis 3:8) Their relationship with God was one of living under God's care and his directives. God did not ask Adam and Eve which way the three of them should live together. God instructed Adam and Eve. Adam and Eve did not instruct God. They were like-minded because they submitted to God's will. And consequently, they reaped an abundance of life from living according to God's purposes, plans, ways and truths.

They lost this wonderful life-giving relationship when they mentally chose to go it alone without God's directives. It was like a divorce. They chose to depart from God's ways in order to live out their own desires in the way they thought best. Remember, the forbidden tree tempted them with the promise of it making them wise so that they would no longer need God's wisdom. (Genesis 3:4-6)

We all wallow in this life and are consumed with death because we, like Adam and Eve, have gone our own way in this world and have missed the ways of God. God describes us as wayward sheep that have wandered and lost their way. Jesus, then, is the good shepherd who gave up his life to bring us back—back into a right relationship with God.

All we like sheep have gone astray; we have turned—every one—to his own way; and the LORD has laid on him the iniquity of us all. Isaiah 53:6 (ESV)

He himself bore our sins in his body on the tree, that **we might die to sin and live to righteousness.** By his wounds you have been healed. For **you were straying like sheep, but have now returned to the Shepherd and Overseer of your souls.** 1 Peter 2:24-25 (ESV)

If we are to come together again with God and become one with him in the way we think, it is not God who is going to conform to our way of thinking. That is death. Our way of thinking is what needs his saving restoration. It is we who will have to change the way we think and conform to God's mind.

Do not be conformed to this present world, but be transformed by the renewing of your mind, so that you may test and approve what is the will of God—what is good and well-pleasing and perfect. Romans 12:2 (NET)

The NLT Bible says, "by changing the way you think". As stated, God wants us to know him, and he wants to know us—on an intimate basis. So what does this intimate relationship look like such that God knows us? God has already chosen to be intimate with us. It was while we were still sinners that he sent his own Son to die for our sins so that our separation from God could be reconciled and this intimate relationship could be restored. (Romans 5:8) But a one-sided relationship does not bring about intimacy; it takes two. God has chosen to adopt us by giving his Holy Spirit to us through the sacrificial life of Jesus Christ. He has chosen to lead us into his paths of life. As we come to him seeking his ways of life, we form an intimate relationship with him as we walk together in the paths he has ordained. This is our love relationship with our Maker.

Good and upright is the LORD; therefore he instructs sinners in the way. He leads the humble in what is right, and teaches the humble his way. All the paths of the LORD are steadfast love and faithfulness, for those who keep his covenant and his testimonies. Psalm 25:8-10 (ESV)

This is our intimate relationship with our heavenly Father. He loves us and he wants us to have his life. He has forgiven our past infringements against him. He forgives us today while we struggle against the sin that is taking our lives. (James 1:13-15) *He loves us, and he does not want to see us wallow in sin and death. Our intimacy with him is one of receiving his life as we seek him and he seeks us. In this pursuit that comes from both sides, we come to know God and he knows us.*

Those who reject this relationship are rejecting God and the life he brings. Jesus is eternal life; so to reject the way of life is to reject Jesus. (1 John 5:11-12) Look at what Jesus said of himself and how this is directly related to our knowing the heavenly Father.

Jesus said to him, "**I am the way, and the truth, and the life. No one comes to the Father except through me. If you had known me**, you would **have known my Father** also. From now on you do know him and have seen him." John 14:6-7 (ESV)

Jesus is the pathway of life. There is only one true life—Jesus. We come to know God and Jesus by seeking Jesus for truth, for he is the embodiment of all truth. *To love God with our minds, we must be seeking this truth with our minds, motivated by our love for knowing God from our hearts. We must then live out this truth so that the life it brings becomes a reality.* That is the meaning of "Jesus is the way". This is how we seek eternal life. This is how we come to know Jesus and our heavenly Father.

Jesus made some very strong and serious statements about entering the kingdom of God and about whether he recognizes us—whether he even knows us.

"Not everyone who says to me, 'Lord, Lord,' will enter into the kingdom of heaven—**only the one who does the will of my Father in heaven**. On that day, many will say to me, 'Lord, Lord, didn't we prophesy in your name, and in your name cast out demons and do many powerful deeds?' Then I will declare to them, **'I never knew you. Go away from me, you lawbreakers!'** Matthew 7:21-23 (NET)

Why did he say, "I never knew you." They called him "Lord, Lord". They prophesied in his name. They cast out demons and other powerful things in the name of Jesus. How could they not know him? It is because they never sought out Jesus to know him and become like him. Jesus is like-minded with his Father. When on earth, he always did the will of his Father. If we are to be like-minded with God, we need to be seeking out God's mind so that we can live out his will in our lives.

Jesus follows this passage with the comparison of our lives to the foundation of a house. The one who seeks to know Jesus' words so that he can put Jesus' teachings into practice in his life is like someone who builds his life on a rock foundation. He will survive the storms of life. But the one who may hear Jesus' words, but does not put them into practice, does not have a solid foundation for his life, and he will not stand when the struggles of life come.

So what can we conclude? How can we sum up what it means to know God and for God to know us? We are lost without God. God wants us to have his life. God longs for us to seek him for his life. He longs for us to know him and for him to know us. We seek him to know him in order to have his wisdom and his character in our lives. This is how we experience his true life. To live in him is to have him live in and through us. If we reject this relationship, we reject God and his life for us, for he is life. *To love God is to choose his life—to seek it and to allow his life to permeate how we think, our attitudes and how we live. This is love for God.*

This is not something new. God has not changed. This call to choose life by following the ways of God has been his calling since the days of his people long ago.

"Today I have given you **the choice between life and death, between blessings and curses.** Now I call on heaven and earth to witness **the choice you make.** Oh, that you would **choose life,** so that you and your descendants might live! **You can make this choice by loving the LORD your God, obeying him, and committing yourself firmly to him. This is the key to your life.** And **if you love and obey the LORD, you will live long in the land** the LORD swore to give your ancestors Abraham, Isaac, and Jacob." Deuteronomy 30:19-20 (NLT)

We make choices with our minds. Our thinking may be driven by our hearts, but decisiveness comes from our minds. What will we choose? Will we chose to love God?

Given the Mind of the Spirit

Without Christ, we wallow around in this world, lost and disconnected from God. How did this all happen? Adam and Eve had daily communication with God. He spoke to them directly. He walked with them in the garden God prepared for them. What happened to this like-minded bond with God? The answer: They decided that they would be better off if they sought their own wisdom rather than God's. The temptation for eating of the forbidden tree had everything to do with their minds. The name of the forbidden tree was "the knowledge of good and evil". They were not eating an apple, as some depict; they were eating of a tree that gave them knowledge, knowledge of good and evil. They were tempted to fill their minds with an understanding that, to this point, was not a part of their thinking. Their existence to this point was one of complete innocence. They had not experienced sin, evil or distrust of any kind. They had never experienced a lie. They never had to wonder or even suspect that what they were told may have been a deception. Their trust in each other and in God was never a question.

But that all changed when the serpent came along. God warned them that if they ate of this tree of the knowledge of good and evil that it would rob them of life; it would kill them. But the serpent said the opposite. He opposed God. "You will not surely die", he said. For the first time, Adam and Eve were confronted with having to consider that someone was lying to them. Either God or the serpent had lied to them. Now they had to choose which one was the liar and which one was telling them the truth. They had to make a choice with their minds. They chose to distrust God and to trust in the serpent—the devil. They also chose to trust their own intellect rather than trust that what God told them was good and that they should obediently adhere to his warnings. Essentially, they chose to disregard God's thinking and serve their own thinking. *This is the essence of the sinful nature, to live life apart from God as our own nature dictates.*

Furthermore, the serpent told them that if they ate of the forbidden tree that it would make them as wise as God. They knew that they had been dependent upon God's wisdom, and now they were tempted with what it would be like to live without God's directives by possessing his wisdom. Of course, this was all a lie. They ate of the forbidden tree, but they never received God's wisdom. Now they were cut off from it.

To this point, they had depended on God's wisdom, now all of mankind walks around, searching for direction. Our lives are continually directed by what we think. We make choices every day. Some choices are simple, such as what to eat or what to wear. Most choices have little consequence on our future. But many of our choices have a great impact on the future. Should I marry? Who should I marry? What career should I pursue? Should I go to college? What job should I take? How should I invest into the future? Should I borrow money for a purchase? Where should I live? The life decisions are endless, and we are all confronted with them.

Now think of a little child. He makes choices too, but for the most part he does not fret about making futuristic choices. He lives under the care of his father and mother. They make all of the big decisions. They look out into the future for their children and determine what should be done. The child just rests in his parent's wisdom, love, protection and care. That was how it was for Adam and Eve before they chose to endeavor out into life on their own with their own wisdom. Their choice to eat of this forbidden tree was one of being independent of God. They knew that they did not have the wisdom needed for venturing out on their own, but a critical part of the temptation came when they were told by the serpent that this tree would make them as wise as God. Take a look at the account.

"You won't die!" the serpent replied to the woman. "God knows that your eyes will be opened as soon as you eat it, and **you will be like God, knowing both good and evil.**"

The woman was convinced. She saw that the tree was beautiful and its fruit looked delicious, and **she wanted the wisdom it would give her.** So she took some of the fruit and ate it. Then she gave some to her husband, who was with her, and he ate it, too. At that moment **their eyes were opened**, and they suddenly felt shame at their nakedness. So they sewed fig leaves together to cover themselves. Genesis 3:4-7 (NLT)

Did they really obtain God's wisdom when they ate of this tree? No, but they did lose their innocence. Prior, they were not knowledgeable about good and evil, but now, sin had entered their existence. They became lost without the wisdom of God to guide them through life. Understand that we all need God's wisdom for life. We are all lost, trying to make the best of this life by depending upon our own thinking. The Scriptures say that we are all like lost sheep that have gone astray, and that Jesus has come as our shepherd to lead us in the way we should go. And just as the devil came to deceive Adam and Eve, he comes to mislead us down a path of destruction and death. But Jesus has come to lead us down his path to an abundant life—eternal life. (John 10:1-18) The key to this life is to return to our dependence on God's wisdom, which he has freely provided by giving us his Spirit.

This is love for God, to seek his mind, his wisdom. Jesus came to restore our relationship with God, the relationship that was lost by the foolish disobedience of Adam and Eve. They chose to hate God. By their actions, they determined that God was a liar and that the devil was telling them the truth. Love for God is to reverse this code of behavior. To love God, we must trust God with his thinking, his wisdom, his commands, and his choices for our lives. To love God we must apply our minds to seek his ways in all of life and then to decide with our minds to follow his instructions. *This is love for God, to make his thoughts our thoughts, and not to expect God to conform to our thoughts and opinions.*

When we become a Christian—when we receive the Spirit of God to literally live within us—we become a new creation. (2 Corinthians 5:17) Our hearts have a new birth. Our minds begin to change at this point, but the change is continuous. It is like enrolling in school for the first time. Entering first grade does not make us instantly intelligent. We have to go through the lengthy and tedious process of education that can take twelve years through high school and possibly many more years of college. And then life after school is a continual education process. The same is true in the process of becoming more and more Christ-like and reaching maturity in Christ. It is a continual growth progression to maturity. And that should be the goal of every Christian, maturity. (Ephesians 4:11-16, Philippians 3:12-16, 1 Corinthians 2:6, Hebrews 5:12-14, James 1:4, 1 Peter 2:1-2, 2 Peter 1:2-11)

There are two aspects of mentally growing in Christ. We can go to school, read all kinds of scholarly Christian books and even memorize scripture verses and religious facts. And there may be great value from being educated in this manner. But this knowledge is of no value if it does not affect the way we think and live. And there is one other aspect of mentally growing in Christ. Education is not the same as having wisdom. Education is not the same as having a spiritual mind. Spiritual life is not intellectually understood; it is understood by having the mind and insight of God. Only God sees things as they truly exist.

The Devil Is Still Planting His Lies

We were born into a dark world, and we were born spiritually blind. We all need the light of Christ and the sight of Christ if we are going to see truth. Satan came into this world as a lying deceiver. He lied to Adam and Eve, and he lies to us. He has the ability to pervert our thinking such that our minds become blind to the truth. Jesus is all truth; he is the bright light of truth. But Satan has blinded us.

If the Good News we preach is hidden behind a veil, it is hidden only from people who are perishing. **Satan, who is the god of this world, has blinded the minds of those who don't believe.** They are unable to see the glorious light of the Good News. **They don't understand this message about the glory of Christ, who is the exact likeness of God**. 2 Corinthians 4:3-4 (NLT)

There is great competition for our minds, what we think and believe. Jesus said that the devil is the Prince of this world. His primary rule is through his influence on what we think. He uses the media, what is written, our culture, the government and any place where our thinking can be influenced. Just the television programming and movies alone have been a powerful force to orchestrate and pervert man's thinking. For example, most shows today revolve around crime or sin of some kind. Most shows portray sex outside of marriage as normal and accepted. Many shows and most TV movies defame the name of God with vulgarities and taking God's name in vain. Many shows portray evolution as a scientific fact, and hide the deceptive theories. If we believed in creation, we would also have to believe in the Creator, God. Most shows either hide God or imply that he does not exist. Many shows teach us that homosexuality is normal, accepted and does not have negative consequences on the person or society. They make it look like a large portion of society is homosexual. A 2015 Gallup poll revealed that, on average, Americans believe that homosexuality consists of about 23% of our population, but the actual is only 3.8%.[3]

> ...but the largest such study by far has been the Gallup Daily tracking measure instituted in June 2012. In this ongoing study, respondents are asked "Do you, personally, identify as lesbian, gay, bisexual or transgender?" with **3.8%** being the most recent result, obtained from more than 58,000 interviews conducted in the first four months of this year.

This same poll measured the change in our moral perception of homosexuality. It is obvious that the "father of all lies", the devil, has been very successful at changing our thinking.

> Whereas 38% of Americans said gay and lesbian relations were morally acceptable in 2002, that number has risen to 63% today *[2015]*. And while 35% of Americans favored legalized same-sex marriage in 1999, 60% favor it today.

This is just one example of how the devil leads our thinking with his deceptions, but there are many more. The devil has been at work to captivate our thinking since the days of Adam and Eve. Jesus came to save us by restoring our sight to know truth and to be a radiant beam of the light of truth. That is why Jesus has given us his Spirit to live within us. By his Spirit we acquire sight and possess the mind of Christ.

> For, "Who can know the LORD's thoughts? Who knows enough to teach him?" But **we understand these things, for we have the mind of Christ**. 1 Corinthians 2:16 (NLT)

---

[3] Newport, Frank. "Americans Greatly Overestimate Percent Gay, Lesbian in U.S."*Gallup.com*. 21 May 2015. Web. 11 Mar. 2016. <http://www.gallup.com/poll/183383/americans-greatly-overestimate-percent-gay-lesbian.aspx>.

The question for us is, "Whom will we love with our minds, God or the devil?" As Jesus stated, eternal life is knowing God and knowing Jesus. (John 17:3) But how can we come to know him if our minds are blind to the wisdom and mind of God? The treasures of God's wisdom and knowledge are hidden in Christ. (Colossians 2:3) And we have been given the Spirit of Christ Jesus so that we, too, can know all of these hidden treasures. It is by the Spirit of God that we are being transformed into the likeness of Jesus Christ through the renewing of our minds.

For those who live according to the flesh **set their minds** on the things of the flesh, but those who live according to the Spirit **set their minds** on the things of the Spirit. For to **set the mind** on the flesh is death, but to **set the mind** on the Spirit is life and peace. For the mind that is set on the flesh is hostile to God, for it does not submit to God's law; indeed, it cannot. Those who are in the flesh cannot please God. Romans 8:5-8 (ESV)

Eternal life is to know the one true God and Jesus Christ. In our own abilities, we are powerless to know God. But the Spirit of God knows God completely, and we have been given the Spirit of wisdom so that we, too, can know God and have eternal life.

I keep asking that the God of our Lord Jesus Christ, the glorious Father, may give you the **Spirit of wisdom and revelation, so that you may know him better**. Ephesians 1:17 (NIV)

Think of what Jesus has done for us. We were lost and separated from God. We were dead in our hearts. We were blind to the wisdom and nature of God. It was impossible for us to know God and to be known by God. That is the downfall of our sinful nature; it cannot know God, nor follow him. So God sent his Spirit to us through Jesus. The Spirit gives us our sight. The Spirit gives us the light we need to see. The Spirit gives us the heart of God.

The Spirit gives us a new mind, unlike the mind of our old nature. The law would have brought life if man could have followed it with his heart and mind. But his heart and mind were corrupted—the essence of our sinful nature. The Spirit of God gives us a new nature, the nature of God.

> The law of Moses was unable to save us because of the weakness of our sinful nature. So God did what the law could not do. He sent his own Son in a body like the bodies we sinners have. And in that body God declared an end to sin's control over us by giving his Son as a sacrifice for our sins. He did this so that the just requirement of the law would be fully satisfied for us, **who no longer follow our sinful nature but instead follow the Spirit**. Romans 8:3-4 (NLT)

Thank God for his Spirit! We now have the mind of Christ. We now have the ability to know God. We now have the ability to recognize what is true and good and to distinguish all of the lies of the devil, the world and our own sinful nature. We now have the ability to pursue true life. We now have the ability to love God with our minds.

Loving God with Our Minds Is a Pursuit

Going to school and becoming educated is an expensive privilege. But just having the opportunity does not mean that we will take full advantage of it. Many students get poor grades. Many drop out of school. Many do not seek higher education so that they will become more valuable citizens. The same can be said for renewing our minds by the power of the Spirit who was freely provided for us through the death of Jesus. We all must still choose to sow to the Spirit for more godly thinking. Wholesome, godly thinking is a pursuit.

> Dear friends, this is now my second letter to you. I have written both of them as reminders to **stimulate you to wholesome thinking**. 2 Peter 3:1 (NIV)

There are many distractions and pressures that can consume our thinking in a wayward direction. Think about it. What is worry? What causes anxiety? Where does fear come from, or negative thinking?

Paul implores us to rest in the Lord, for he is near and loves us. His purposes will prevail, and God is all powerful. Instead of being anxious, we should beckon God to come to our aid. We should use our minds to focus on what God has done and what he has promised for those he loves. We need to transform our complaining to thanksgiving. And if we do, we will have the peace of God and he will guard our hearts and minds.

> Rejoice in the Lord always. Again I say, rejoice! Let everyone see your gentleness. The Lord is near! Do not be anxious about anything. Instead, in every situation, through prayer and petition with thanksgiving, tell your requests to God. And **the peace of God that surpasses all understanding will guard your hearts and minds in Christ Jesus**.
>
> Finally, brothers and sisters, **whatever is true, whatever is worthy of respect, whatever is just, whatever is pure, whatever is lovely, whatever is commendable, if something is excellent or praiseworthy, think about these things**. Philippians 4:4-8 (NET)

It is our choice regarding what we think about. What we think about is a conscious choice. Does that sound like an oxymoron? We need to think about what we choose to think about, and then think about such things.

We do have a choice. Our old sinful nature tugs at us in one direction, and the Spirit of God in the opposite direction. We sit between these two forces and can decide which one to serve with our minds. If we sow to the Spirit, we will reap joy, peace and contentment. If we sow to the sinful nature, we will reap discontent, anxiety, fear and worry. If we love ourselves and if we truly love God, there is really only one choice! And it all hinges on how we are taught and the attitude of our minds.

Surely you heard of him and were **taught in him in accordance with the truth that is in Jesus.** You were **taught, with regard to your former way of life,** to put off your old self, which is being corrupted by its deceitful desires; **to be made new in the attitude of your minds;** and to **put on the new self, created to be like God in true righteousness and holiness.** Ephesians 4:21-24 (NIV)

To love God with our minds is to hunger for his mind, to hunger for his way of living, which is the only true life—eternal life.

Blessed are those who hunger and thirst for righteousness, for they will be filled. Matthew 5:6 (NIV)

Reflection Questions

Do you worry or fret about life? Describe your struggle and what you worry about. What would it be like if God literally lived in your house with you on a daily basis? Would you fret and worry? Why do you fret and worry now?

How do you apply your mind to think as God would think in all situations?

Describe your intimacy with God in how you are like-minded with his thinking.

Have you been born again of the Spirit of God? What is the testimony of his Spirit within you regarding the change of your thinking? Give specific examples of how you used to think and how you think now.

Describe how you pursue God's way of thinking by the study of his word and how you apply it to your life.

Chapter 7

Washed by the Word

We live in a physical and spiritual world. We all can sense the physical world. It is continually observed by what we see, hear, smell, taste and feel. We do not require any proof of its existence, and we all perceive its enormity and complexities. But what about the spiritual world? It is just as real, but we cannot witness its existence with our five senses. We can all sense our own thoughts and emotions, which are spiritual, but the spiritual realm goes far beyond our individual beings. Fortunately, there are many parallels between the physical and spiritual realms. God has given us many physical experiences and perceptions so that we can begin to get an understanding of spiritual realities that are beyond our senses. The Bible is filled with them. For example, the Old Testament temple pointed ahead to the eternal, spiritual temple, and we are that temple. And the sacrifice of animals for the sins of the people pointed ahead to the sacrifice of Jesus for forgiveness of our sins. Or, another example, our marriages give us an understanding of the unity between a husband and wife, which gives us a picture of our eternal marriage between Jesus and his bride, the body of Christ. Or, how could we understand the kingdom of God if we had not experienced the kingdoms (nations) of the earth?

The Bible talks about being washed by the Word of God. What does that mean? Becoming dirty and feeling the need to wash to become clean is another example of our physical existence pointing ahead to the spiritual. We all get dirty and smelly; and we all know what it means to seek cleansing. In the United States, we feel dirty if we do not shower at least once per day.

Of course, we are talking about the cleansing of our bodies. What about our minds? Our minds are part of our spiritual bodies. Can our minds become dirty? Think about a "dirty joke"? What makes a joke dirty? It is not because the joke contains reference to physical filth. It is because there are certain things in life that we define as filthy. Things like sexual deviancy are a common source for a "dirty joke". How about "dirty words". Taking the Lord's name in vane is considered dirty. So is the use of foul language such as the F... word.

We are all familiar with something that is physically dirty and something being spiritually dirty. God defines what is clean—spiritual cleanness. *We love God by pursing spiritual cleanliness*. Being spiritually clean has nothing to do with physically cleanliness. It has everything to do with being clean inside—spiritually clean.

The Pharisees were overly concerned about how they appeared outwardly, but they were oblivious to their inward filth. Jesus accepted all sorts of spiritually dirty people—demon possessed, adulterers, tax collectors—most anyone. He accepted them because they knew they were in need of a cleansing inside. But there was one group whom he did not accept, the proud Pharisees. They hid the dirt on the inside by presenting a holy and righteous exterior. Jesus did not mince words with them. He spoke directly to their hypocrisy.

"Woe to you, scribes and Pharisees, hypocrites! You clean the outside of the cup and dish, but inside they are full of greed and self-indulgence! Blind Pharisee! First clean the inside of the cup, so the outside of it may also become clean.

"Woe to you, scribes and Pharisees, hypocrites! You are like whitewashed tombs, which appear beautiful on the outside, but inside are full of dead men's bones and every impurity. In the same way, on the outside you seem righteous to people, but inside you are full of hypocrisy and lawlessness. Matthew 23:25-28 (HCSB)

Pride is a cover-up for what is truly inside of a person. But there is another cover-up that may be equally unseen by ourselves. Our traditions and practices can fool us into thinking that we are clean on the inside, when in actuality, nothing has changed within us or in our daily lives and relationships. Going to church on Sundays, wearing a cross necklace, having an identity by having affiliations with particular groups, speaking the right Christian lingo, knowing all of the right biblical answers and intellect, praying aloud with all of the "right" words and many other outward practices and identities may have some benefits, but can also have no effect on the inner man. The outward man may have the appearance of being clean, but the inner man is still dirty.

The Pharisees were blind to their own pride, and they were also blind to the lifeless pursuit of their traditions. Jesus addressed them directly. (Mark 7:1-23) He makes it very clear that outward activities do not change the heart and mind of man. Rather, a change to the heart and mind will change the outward behaviors and attitudes to conform to the righteousness of Jesus. Here is an excerpt of his words and his explanation to his disciples.

Nothing outside a man can make him 'unclean' by going into him. Rather, it is what comes out of a man that makes him 'unclean.' "

After he had left the crowd and entered the house, his disciples asked him about this parable. "Are you so dull?" he asked. "Don't you see that nothing that enters a man from the outside can make him 'unclean'? For it doesn't go into his heart but into his stomach, and then out of his body." (In saying this, Jesus declared all foods "clean.")

He went on: "What comes out of a man is what makes him 'unclean.' **For from within, out of men's hearts, come evil thoughts, sexual immorality, theft, murder, adultery, greed, malice, deceit,**

lewdness, envy, slander, arrogance and folly. All these evils come from inside and make a man 'unclean.'" Mark 7:15-23 (NIV)

So how do we wash the inner man, the mind and heart?

Spiritual Cleansing

Recognizing that we are dirty followed by taking a bath is something we deliberately and consciously do. It is an act of our will. Most of us have a discipline of taking a shower once a day. We brush our teeth several times a day. And we routinely wash our hands. In like manner, we need to cleanse our mind with the word of God to keep our mind, heart and soul clean. We need to recognize when we are spiritually dirty so we can take a spiritual bath. How do we recognize spiritual filth in us? How do we take a spiritual bath?

I think of myself before becoming a Christ follower. My language was filthy, but I was oblivious to my offensive vulgarities. I was racially prejudiced, but I saw no wrong in it because I was brought up (trained) to be prejudiced by my extended family who regularly spoke out against and exaggerated the shortcomings of the blacks. I was led into pornography and the pursuit of sexual pleasures by my older brother when I was very young. I saw no wrong in my sexual satisfactions. The filth of my soul was disgusting, but I could not see my dirt.

Then one day, in my late twenties, God led me into his word. I wasn't looking for anything other than substantiating my own opinions and beliefs about life. I had my own beliefs and opinions, and I was sure that the Bible would agree with my perceptions. What actually happened was totally unexpected. I was filthy inside, and God was giving me a bath. He was in the process of cleaning my mind and my heart.

The word of God is like soap and water that emulsifies the filth to lift it from the mind and then rinse it from the soul and flush it down into the sewer where it belongs. This is the saving power of Jesus Christ. He is not coming for a filthy bride; he is coming for a "bride that has made herself ready" with "fine linen, bright and clean". (Revelation 19:7-8) And he has given us his word to cleanse us.

> Husbands, love your wives, just as Christ loved the church and gave Himself for her **to make her holy, cleansing her with the washing of water by the word**. He did this to present the church to Himself in splendor, without spot or wrinkle or anything like that, but holy and blameless. Ephesians 5:25-27 (HCSB)

What bride would come to the wedding smelly and dirty? No, she spends months preparing what she will wear. Her dress is white and flowing. Her hair is done to bring forth her maximum beauty. Her adornment is prepared to bring her husband pleasure from the sight of her white, shining attraction. She loves her husband, and he loves her. They are about to commit themselves to love one another for the rest of their lives. We are the bride of Christ. As his bride, we are to please him with our beauty. His word makes us clean and beautiful as it is applied to our lives.

Jesus is the groom and we are the bride. We become one with each other. Jesus gives us another picture of our union with him. He is the vine and we are the branches. Fruit finds its source of nutrition by being connected to the tree. It blossoms, grows and matures as it receives all that it needs from the tree that supports it. The goal of our faith in Christ should be to bear him fruit—the fruit of his Spirit, the Spirit that has been freely given to us. That is God's primary goal for our lives. *If we are to love God, bearing fruit for him should be our goal as well. Without the cleansing of our minds and hearts by his word, we will not bear fruit for God*. The word of God cleanses us so that we can bear much fruit to the glory of God.

> "I am the true vine, and My Father is the vineyard keeper. Every branch in Me that does not produce fruit He removes, and He prunes every branch that produces fruit so that it will produce more fruit. **You are already clean because of the word I have spoken to you**. Remain in Me, and I in you. Just as a branch is unable to produce fruit by itself

unless it remains on the vine, so neither can you unless you remain in Me.

"I am the vine; you are the branches. The one who remains in Me and I in him produces much fruit, because you can do nothing without Me. If anyone does not remain in Me, he is thrown aside like a branch and he withers. They gather them, throw them into the fire, and they are burned. If you remain in Me and My words remain in you, ask whatever you want and it will be done for you. **My Father is glorified by this: that you produce much fruit and prove to be My disciples**. John 15:1-8 (HCSB)

Without the washing by his word and the flow of his Spirit, we cannot bear fruit for God; we are incapable of loving God.

How Do We Cleanse?

Occasionally, we will have a smudge on our face, but unless we look in the mirror, we are unaware. Someone may tell us, but we may not believe them. We have to see it for ourselves in the mirror. The same is true for the filth of our souls. We need a mirror to reveal the truth about our inner being. We need it to bring the hidden things from our soul out into the conscious reality of our minds. But where do we find a mirror for the soul? God has given us the word of God. It is more than a book; it is a living mirror for our decaying souls.

For the word of God is alive and powerful. It is sharper than the sharpest two-edged sword, cutting between soul and spirit, between joint and marrow. **It exposes our innermost thoughts and desires.** Nothing in all creation is hidden from God. Everything is naked and exposed before his eyes, and he is the one to whom we are accountable. Hebrews 4:12-13 (NLT)

Most Americans shower once a day. We don't necessarily see the dirt on our bodies. Much of the time we are cleansing oils, films, odors and germs that are out of sight. We just feel grimy, and a hot shower feels good. We don't wait several days for someone to tell us about our body odor or to remark about our greasy hair. We are preemptive and keep our bodies clean on a daily basis.

So how can we be preemptive about keeping our souls clean? It begins by keeping our minds clean—giving our minds a daily bath.

The word of God is what brought me out of darkness and into the saving light of the Spirit of Christ. I have a very high regard for the power of God in his written word for us. Just like taking a hot shower every day, I spend time reading the cleansing word on a daily basis. Just like I take a shower to start my day, I read his word before entering the activities of the day. I do not remember missing the bathing of my soul with God's word. It has likely been several decades since missing a day to cleanse my mind and soul. I don't seek his word out of pride, shame, judgment, legalism or any compulsion to be acceptable. I seek his word because the filth of the world and my sinful nature has the power to destroy my life and my relationship with God. I do not want to lose what he has already been freely given to me; it is too valuable—it is life.

Many years ago, when my children were young, (We have nine of them.) I knew that they needed to bath their souls daily if they were to have life from God. If I had a daily spiritual bath from childhood, I would not have lived such a filthy life for my first thirty years. I wanted my household to be different; I wanted to make his word ever present in our whole family. It was very much a part of our household, coming from my wife and me, but we cannot bath our children forever. Eventually, they needed to be bathing themselves. I taught them and encouraged them to read and pray daily on their own. I encouraged them in a daily discipline by giving each of them a one page calendar with a place to mark where they read each day. I promised them $100 to read ten minutes and pray five minutes every day. They could miss two days in the year without losing any money. After that, they forfeited $5 for every day missed. We have nine children. This promotion began when they were about eight and lasted until they were eighteen. That's ten years for each of nine kids at $100 every year. That is a potential of $9,000, and rarely did anyone miss a day, and without any prompting by their mother or me. I have paid out thousands of dollars, and every dollar was well invested. They are all adults now. Most are married and have their own families. And all nine are well versed in God's word. All nine know God and live according to his ways. None have gone wayward as I did when I was young. And for the most part, they have continued to bath themselves with the word as adults.

Staying Out of the Mud

Just knowing that we are dirty is of no value if we do not then wash off the filth. Usually, after taking a shower, we put on clean clothes and set the smelly, dirty ones aside for the washing machine. Why take a bath if we are just going to put the same dirty clothes back on? And who takes a bath, knowing that he is immediately going out to do some dirty, sweaty work?

How does that compare to the washing of our minds and souls? We can read God's word without the intent of becoming clean. We can read it intellectually for head knowledge, without the practice of applying what we read to our lives. Actually, we can fool ourselves into thinking that just by having a bathing room that we are then clean. No, to become clean we have to become immersed, and to become immersed we have to apply what we see and learn from his word to our lives—the way we think, our attitudes and our behaviors.

This is when our love for God becomes a reality. Think about it; God wants us to have his life. There is no other life; God is it. He has given us his word to cleanse us from all the things that rob us of life. *If we love God, we will desire his life. If we desire his life we will seek truth from Jesus, the way of life, God's word. And if we love his life, we will apply what he freely gives us.* How can someone think that he loves God, but then ignores his word and does not apply his life-giving transformations to the way we think and live? And if we know his word, but do not apply it, are we not just like the hypocritical Pharisees? We can easily be deceived because we call ourselves Christians and go to church services. But reality is proven in the way we live, moment by moment. The evidence is revealed by the fruit we bare. (Matthew 7:17-23) We can deceive ourselves by having a devotional time but not really having a cleansing.

> But be doers of the word, and not hearers only, **deceiving yourselves**. For if anyone is a hearer of the word and not a doer, he is like a man who looks intently at his natural face in a mirror. For he looks at himself and goes away and at once forgets what he was like. But the one who looks into the perfect law, the law of liberty, and perseveres, being no hearer who forgets but a doer who acts, he will be blessed in his doing. James 1:22-25 (ESV)

That was James's instruction. Jesus was just as adamant of the importance of seeking to hear his word and then to apply his word to our lives. In other words, we need to decisively seek to know his word for the purpose of a changed mind and life. So, after studying his word, we then need to deliberately apply what we have learned.

> "Everyone who hears these words of mine and does them is like a wise man who built his house on rock. The rain fell, the flood came, and the winds beat against that house, but it did not collapse because it had been founded on rock. Everyone who hears these words of mine and does not do them is like a foolish man who built his house on sand. The rain fell, the flood came, and the winds beat against that house, and it collapsed; it was utterly destroyed!" Matthew 7:24-27 (NET)

Seeking God's word and then applying it to our lives is loving God. This is not about feeling love for God; this is about loving God. He is not looking at our emotions; he is looking for the fruit of a wholesome, godly life as we discover the way of life from the truth of his word and then walk accordingly.

We know that we have come to know him if we obey his commands. **The man who says, "I know him," but does not do what he commands is a liar, and the truth is not in him.** But if anyone obeys his word, God's love is truly made complete in him. This is how we know we are in him: **Whoever claims to live in him must walk as Jesus did.** 1 John 2:3-6 (NIV)

Meditating On the Word

So we see that to love God we must be in pursuit of becoming like God in the way we think—the way we see life—the way we know God—and the way we live our lives. This pursuit begins with how we think. And if we desire to think as God thinks, we must have his wisdom living within us. The source is twofold: The Spirit of Christ and the word of God. Jesus was sent by God so that we would have his wisdom; we would have the mind of God, and therefore the life of God living within us. (1 Corinthians 1:30, Romans 8:5-8) Jesus has sent his Spirit to live within us, and by his Spirit we can see God and life from God's perspective. But just having his Spirit is not a pursuit. The pursuit comes from deliberately seeking to know God and truth. God has given us his Spirit, but he has also given us his holy word. The transformation of our minds requires of us to meditate on his word. Mediation is not spending hours reciting verses over and over to ourselves. Mediation is applying our minds to discover the hidden truths of life. God is life; he defines life. Jesus is the word of God. Jesus is the embodiment of truth. Jesus is the path that leads to life. Jesus is eternal life. (John 14:6) We meditate on his word to discover truth, the way to live and life itself. It is a transformation of our minds, and from this transformation we have the power to live a new life. This pursuit is love for God.

The world, as led by the devil, is in competition for our minds. He feeds our thinking from a multitude of sources. The many facets of media are filled with his ungodly views. He enters our school classrooms and is on the pages of many of our books. He dominates our culture and dictates what is considered normal. He speaks directly to us by the people he directs into our lives.

To love God with our minds requires of us to avoid the teachings of the world and to pursue the wisdom of God found in the word of God.

Blessed is the man who walks not in the counsel of the wicked, nor stands in the way of sinners, nor sits in the seat of scoffers; but his delight is in the law of the LORD, and on his law **he meditates day and night**. He is like a tree planted by streams of water that yields its fruit in its season, and its leaf does not wither. In all that he does, he prospers. Psalm 1:1-3 (ESV)

The world is all around us. We can refrain from watching television and avoid certain places and people, but we cannot leave this world in which the devil reigns. But we can meditate on God's word so that the light of his truth has the opportunity to dispel the darkness around us. Jesus instructs—even warns us—to make sure that we have his light within us.

See to it, then, that the light within you is not darkness. Luke 11:35 (NIV)

If we are to have his light within us, we need to seek the light of his word so that it lives within us as a bright light. If we are not meditating on his word, we will not have his light, and without light, we have darkness. The psalmist talks about this pursuit, not as a legalistic burden, but as a life-giving delight.

I will **study your commandments** and **reflect on your ways**. I will **delight in your decrees** and **not forget your word**. Psalm 119:15-16 (NLT)

Yes, I have **more insight** than my teachers, for I am **always thinking of your laws**. Psalm 119:99 (NLT)

Make me **understand the way of your precepts**, and I will **meditate on your wondrous works**. Psalm 119:27 (ESV)

To love God is to meditate on God's laws, God's wisdom for us, on God's promises to us, on God's marvelous works, on God's power and character. This is not an academic work, like going to school, although much learning occurs. This is more like searching for hidden treasure. We are driven to find the secrets and power of life itself. What we find is what all mankind truly wants, but they have been blinded by the world and do not know that true peace, joy, and happiness—true life—are found in God by searching out his word to us. This is the motivation of the psalmist when he talks about meditating on God's word.

My eyes stay open through the watches of the night, that I may **meditate on your promises**. Psalm 119:148 (NIV)

On the glorious splendor of your majesty, and on your wondrous works, I will meditate. Psalm 145:5 (ESV)

We **reflect on your loyal love**, O God, within your temple. Psalm 48:9 (NET)

I will **ponder all your work**, and **meditate on your mighty deeds**. Psalm 77:12 (ESV)

To love God with our minds is a pursuit of our minds to know God, to know his wisdom, to know his ways of living, to know his love, to know his heart, to see life as he sees it, to think as God thinks—to have the mind of Christ.

For, "Who can know the LORD's thoughts? Who knows enough to teach him?" But we understand these things, for **we have the mind of Christ**. 1 Corinthians 2:16 (NLT)

Reflection Questions

How well do you know God's word? Have you read the entire Bible, from Genesis to Revelation?

What is your daily Bible reading discipline?

What is your practice of meditating on the Word?

How has your life changed as a result of your study?

What spiritual dirt has been cleansed from you? And how are you becoming more beautiful for God?

Chapter 8

Artificial Love for God

As a marriage counselor, I once had a man call me in desperation. His wife was filing for divorce. She was leaving him after many years of marriage, and he was devastated. He asked if he could meet with me. I expected him to come alone, but his wife decided to come too, and it was good that she did so that I could get the full and truthful picture. He had a restaurant, and he worked many long hours, leaving his wife alone at home. Then when he took time away from work, he pursued activities without his wife. He even took vacations without her. She was a forgotten, ignored spouse who was just there to fill his house when he was home.

The husband sobbed and pleaded with her: "I love you! I love you!" "Please don't leave me." I had to stop him in his false confessions: "You do not, and have not, loved your wife. You are just feeling the pain of her rejection of you and the loss of her not being there for you. That is not love for her. That is the pain of your own loss." I offered to meet with him to show him what real love looked like as described in God's word. He never took me up on my offer. He really did not love his wife. He wanted his wife to love him, but he did not want to love his wife.

Wonderful Feelings Are Not the Same as Love

God wants us to love him, and just like this man, we can become confused as to what loving him really means. Sometimes we may think we love God, but we are really reflecting on how it makes us feel when we recognize his love and our need for his love. That is not the same as loving God.

When we meet the man or woman of our dreams, we "fall in love". What does that mean? The Bible doesn't talk about love that way—"falling in love". Most of us have had this experience. All that we want to do is to be with our newfound love mate. We can talk for hours, just enjoying each other's presence. What is going on inside? Is this love? Well, it is love in that we are feeling the overwhelming connection with a man or woman. And it is a blessing to the other person to hear, "I love you." But this is not Biblical love. Biblically, to love someone is to give up part of my life for the benefit of someone else's life. Jesus said that the greatest love is for someone to give up his life for his friend. (John 15:13) He also told us to love our enemies and those who abuse us and those who persecute us. He told us to pray for them. (Matthew 5:38-48) He instructs us to take up our cross daily. In other words, do not retaliate against those who harm you. Rather, forgive them. (Luke 9:21-25) This kind of love is not filled with all of those infatuation feelings that may be felt between a man and a woman when they first "fall in love". Biblical love is sacrificial. We love because it is right and because we care—whether we get something in return or not. It is not based on the good feelings that we get out of it. In fact, the "fall in love" attraction is mostly self-gratifying. It feels so good that you want more and more of it. Remove the feelings, and then what is the love for the other person like? That is the real test of our love!

Don't get me wrong; it is great to have these feelings for the one we love. It would be wonderful if every married couple could maintain such wonderful feelings of attraction for forty, fifty, sixty years or more of marriage. But these feelings usually subside in just months. The "fall in love" syndrome is mostly based on a dream of how wonderful the other person makes me feel. We see the beauty of the other person, but we only actually know about five percent of who they really are. We fill in the other ninety-five percent with our imaginary perfection. Then, after marriage, we begin to discover the real ninety-five percent, and it is not as dreamily perfect as we once perceived. Now we have to love that person for who they really are. We also begin to discover the reign of our own selfishness. And if we do love them for who they are, that is true love.

Another reason these infatuation feelings fade is because we begin to get bored with each other. In the "fall in love" stage, we spend all of our time and energy with this one person, ignoring all of the other things we like to do. We give up everything else for this one person because it feels so good. But after marriage, we crave to fill our lives back up with our own desires and needs. So our spouse does not get all of the time and attention that they received in the "fall in love" stage.

It should be obvious that "falling in love" is mostly about a pursuit of the good feelings we receive from the relationship with the opposite sex. It is not about giving up for the other person. Although we may feel like we would give up anything at the time. The real drive is about receiving from the other person. The feelings are deceptive. They make us feel like we would do anything for the other person. And as long as the feelings remain, we probably would. But when the self gratifying feelings disappear, so does the love with all of its sacrificial attributes. This is not biblical love, and it is not the kind of love that God desires of us.

True Love Is Not an Outward Form or Expression

I frequently hear professions from people regarding how much they love God. In a worship setting they are animated with the raising of their hands and possibly with tears in their eyes. A first impression may be that this has to be someone who loves God. But we can be fooled, thinking that we love God because we appreciate God for who he is and what he has done for us. Do not misunderstand me; thanksgiving, appreciation and worship are an important aspect of our loving relationship with God. Our expression of who God is and what he has done out of love for us is very much a part of our love relationship with God. We are clearly told to praise him with a thankful heart and with a heartfelt expression of his greatness.

Praise the LORD, all nations! Extol him, all peoples! For great is his steadfast love toward us, and the faithfulness of the LORD endures forever. Praise the LORD! Psalm 117:1-2 (ESV)

Expressing how God loves us blesses God; just as the thankful expressions of our child blesses us. But what if that same child, who expressed all the right things, then lived a wayward life, opposed to the instructions and guidance of his father? What if he went his own way, getting involved in deviant behaviors, failing in school and hanging out with others who also lived deliberate sinful lives. How much love does that child really have for his father, in spite of his appreciative words?

It is fully possible to feel God's love for us without returning love back to him. *Feeling his love for us is not the same as our love for him.*

The true test of our love for God is not on Sunday morning. The true test is how we think, feel and act all seven days a week in every environment, every relationship and every situation we find ourselves. The true test of our love for God is when we are being tested.

The sovereign master says, "These people say they are loyal to me; they say wonderful things about me, but they are not really loyal to me. Their worship consists of nothing but man-made ritual. Isaiah 29:13 (NET)

True authentic love for God is revealed in how we live our lives. For example, we may worship God with our lips on Sunday morning or when we are listening to praise music on our ear phones, but then we complain about our lives with these same lips, or we hurt someone with our words, or we lie or we gossip. Do we love God? Look at what Jesus' brother wrote about our tongue.

With it we bless our Lord and Father, and with it we curse people who are made in the likeness of God. From the same mouth come blessing and cursing. My brothers, these things ought not to be so. Does a spring pour forth from the same opening both fresh and salt water? Can a fig tree, my brothers, bear olives, or a grapevine produce figs? Neither can a salt pond yield fresh water. James 3:9-12 (ESV)

If someone thinks he is religious yet does not bridle his tongue, and so deceives his heart, his religion is futile. Pure and undefiled religion before God the Father is this: to care for orphans and widows in their misfortune and to keep oneself unstained by the world. James 1:26-27 (NET)

A true relationship with God is not about participation in religious activities. It is not about having a religious affiliation with a church or other group. It is not about wearing a Christian T-shirt, or having the right bumper sticker, or wearing a cross necklace. An authentic love relationship with God is borne out in how we live our lives. Mainly it is how we love other people. Living in sin opposes our love for God.

Hypocrites Are Deceived

Through prison ministry I have known many men who have lived daily criminal lives for decades. In prison, Jesus humbled them and got their attention. I have witnessed their thinking, attitudes and behaviors, and they clearly reveal a man who has been saved by Jesus Christ. But it is common for these same men to proclaim that they became a Christian back in the days when they were pursuing an evil life. Their mouths spewed profanity and vulgarities. They took and sold drugs. They had sex on a regular basis outside of marriage. They conned and manipulated others. They hated people. They violently assaulted and abused others. But they thought they were Christians because one day they got baptized, or because their aunt took them to church occasionally. But they never repented of their sinful life and they never worshiped God with their lives. They never loved God.

The Pharisees knew and recited God's word. They were a very religious group. But they did not know God, and neither did they love God. As Christians we look down on the Pharisees, and rightly so. But we can be fooled in our own hearts, like the Pharisees who thought that they loved God because of their religious practices and their godly words. Jesus was not fooled by their hypocrisy.

You hypocrites! Isaiah was right when he prophesied about you: "'These people honor me with their lips, but their hearts are far from me. They worship me in vain; their teachings are but rules taught by men.'" Matthew 15:7-9 (NIV)

A hypocrite is someone who professes one thing with his lips, but his life tells a different story. Jesus also accused these Pharisees of being blind. They were so blind that they could not see the truth about themselves; they were hypocrites who did not truly love God. They saw their religious practices as love for God, but they ignored the commands of God for their own behaviors. We all need to examine our lives. Are we hypocrites?

This deceptive, hypocritical view of love for God is not new. God was continually upset and hurt by the hypocritical attitudes and practices of his people. They thought that because they had the temple of God and because they went into the temple to worship, that their relationship with God was in good standing. They completely missed that God wanted their lives, not their religious practices, which only required a few hours of their time each week. God was not vague about what they were doing, about their hypocritical worship of him.

The LORD said to Jeremiah: "Stand in the gate of the LORD's temple and proclaim this message: 'Listen, all you people of Judah who have passed through these gates to worship the LORD. Hear what the LORD has to say. The LORD God of Israel who rules over all says: **Change the way you have been living and do what is right**. If you do, I will allow you to continue to live in this land. **Stop putting your** confidence in the false belief that says, "We are safe! The temple of the LORD is here! The temple of the LORD is here! The temple of the LORD is here!" You must change the way you have been living and do what is right. You must treat one another fairly. Stop oppressing foreigners who live in your land, children who have lost their fathers, and women who have lost their husbands. Stop killing innocent people in this land. Stop paying allegiance to other gods. That will only bring about your ruin. If you stop doing these things, I will allow you to continue to live in this land which I gave to your ancestors as a lasting possession.

"'But just look at you! You are putting your confidence in a false belief that will not deliver you. You steal. You murder. You commit adultery. You lie when you swear on oath. You sacrifice to the god Baal. You pay allegiance to other gods whom you have not previously known. Then you come and stand in my presence in this temple I have claimed as my own and say, "We are safe!" You think you are so safe that you go on doing all those hateful sins! Do you think this temple I have claimed as my own is to be a hideout for robbers? You had better take note! I have seen for myself what you have done! says the LORD. Jeremiah 7:1-11 (NET)

Paul wrote to the Galatians, "Do not be deceived: God cannot be mocked." (Galatians 6:7) Paul is warning us, do not be deceived. God knows the difference between our professions of love for him and true love, which is living our lives for him. He is not fooled by hypocrisy, but we can be easily fooled by our own hearts. Feelings are great, but feelings are not necessarily for God. Wonderful feelings make us feel good. If we truly want God to find pleasure in us, we need to live for him.

Giving God What Is Leftover

The children of Israel were commanded to sacrifice unto God their "firstfruits". In other words, they were not to give him what was left over.

They were not to give him what was blemished or depleted by any means. They were not to give to God after they had given to themselves. They were to give to him what was first and best, and then they could serve themselves with the rest. (Exodus 23:14-19, 34:18-26, Leviticus 2:11-15, 23:15-22, and several other references)

> Honor the LORD with your wealth, with the firstfruits of all your crops; then your barns will be filled to overflowing, and your vats will brim over with new wine. Proverbs 3:9-10 (NIV)

In essence, God wants our very best, a portion of all of our lives. He wants the first of our money, of our time, of our talents and abilities, of our energy, of our possessions—of anything that is associated with our lives. He wants to be the top priority of our lives.

The priests of old made their required sacrifices to God, but they did not offer their best—their firstfruits. They thought that God would be pleased with their offerings, just because it was an offering. But their offerings were detestable to God because they were not their best. God does not want to be given what is left over.

> "A son honors his father, and a servant his master. If then I am a father, **where is my honor**? And if I am a master, **where is my fear**? says the LORD of hosts to you, O priests, who despise my name. But you say, 'How have we despised your name?' By offering polluted food upon my altar. But you say, 'How have we polluted you?' By saying that the LORD's table may be despised. **When you offer blind animals in sacrifice, is that not evil? And when you offer those that are lame or sick, is that not evil?** Present that to your governor; will he accept you or show you favor? says the LORD of hosts. And now entreat the favor of God, that he may be gracious to us. With such a gift from your hand, will he show favor to any of you? says the LORD of hosts. Oh that there were one among you who would shut the doors, that you might not kindle fire on my altar in vain! **I have no pleasure in you, says the**

LORD of hosts, and I will not accept an offering from your hand. For from the rising of the sun to its setting my name will be great among the nations, and in every place incense will be offered to my name, and a pure offering. For my name will be great among the nations, says the LORD of hosts. But you profane it when you say that the Lord's table is polluted, and its fruit, that is, its food may be despised. But you say, 'What a weariness this is,' and you snort at it, says the LORD of hosts. You bring what has been taken by violence or is lame or sick, and this you bring as your offering! Shall I accept that from your hand? says the LORD. **Cursed be the cheat who has a male in his flock, and vows it, and yet sacrifices to the Lord what is blemished**. For I am a great King, says the LORD of hosts, and my name will be feared among the nations. Malachi 1:6-14 (ESV)

It may seem that God is pleased with whatever we offer him, but that was certainly not the case. We need to see our relationship with God as a marriage where God is our husband, and we are his wife. God is a jealous God, and he wants to be our only lover. He wants us to seek him and give ourselves to him as our first desire and choice.

As God's people, he does not want to share us. He wants our best. Imagine a wife who gives herself to others in adultery, but also offers her sexual pleasures to her husband. Would her husband be pleased? Would he feel loved by her? Or would he detest her sexual pleasures out of jealousy and anger.

Okay, that may seem like an extreme example. But do we offer ourselves to the world with most of our heart, soul, mind and strength, and then give God a few hours or activities out of our week and expect him to be delighted in our offering?

God wants the most and the first of us. He does not want to share our love with anyone or anything else. He is to be our first priority. He does not consent to being in any other place than first place.

Imagine a husband who spends sixty, eighty or even one hundred hours at work because of his love for his career. What wife would not be hurt, jealous and angry? Imagine a wife who gives most of her time and attention to her children and grandchildren, typically leaving her husband as a second choice or priority. Will he feel loved, enjoyed, appreciated, honored and respected when he gets what is left over from his wife's time, attention and energy?

If we are to love God at all, he must be a first priority. He demands our first fruits. Nothing else will please him. The giving of leftovers is not really true love. We know this about our earthly marriages, and God knows it in his marriage with us.

We Cannot Love Both God and the World

For the most part, loving God consists of obeying his command to love others. It means that we pursue his righteous ways of living and refrain from the ways of the world and our own sinful desires. Without these basic ingredients, our love for God is probably just a nice feeling or a stand that we take to feel safe and accepted in his presence. We should take warning: we can be easily deceived. If we do not love others, we cannot love God. If we love the world, we cannot also love God.

Do not love this world nor the things it offers you, for when you love the world, you do not have the love of the Father in you. For the world offers only a craving for physical pleasure, a craving for everything we see, and pride in our achievements and possessions. These are not from the Father, but are from this world. And this world is fading away, along with everything that people crave. But **anyone who does what pleases God will live forever**. 1 John 2:15-17 (NLT)

Loving God is a choice; just as loving our spouse is a choice. We cannot have an adulterous relationship with our neighbor and then profess that we love our spouse. True love is mutually exclusive. God says that he is a jealous god, to the extent that he says his name is Jealous. (Exodus 34:14) God is jealous of our love for the things of the world. We cannot have affairs with the world all week and then come home to God on Sunday and profess how much we love him. "Without faith it is impossible to please God". (Hebrews 6:6) In faith, we love God. In faith we abstain from loving the world. This is our faithfulness to God.

> **This is love for God: to obey his commands**. And his commands are not burdensome, for **everyone born of God overcomes the world**. This is the victory that has overcome the world, **even our faith**. 1 John 5:3-4 (NIV)

Loving God and Hating Others Are Opposites

Notice that John defines love for God as obeying his commands. And Jesus' primary command for our lives is to love those who are in our lives. (John 13:34-35, 1 John 3:21-24) If we say that we love God, we must also love others. We cannot hate someone and then say that we love God. If we love God we will obey his command to love.

> We love because he first loved us. **If anyone says, "I love God," and hates his brother, he is a liar**; for he who does not love his brother whom he has seen cannot love God whom he has not seen. And this commandment we have from him: **whoever loves God must also love his brother**. 1 John 4:19-21 (ESV)

Compartmentalizing our Love for God

There are many ways in which we can fool ourselves into thinking that we love God. The deception comes when we categorize our lives. We set aside certain times and religious activity for God and then we set apart the rest of our lives as belonging to us. To truly love God is to offer our lives for his purposes. We cannot come to him, tell him we love him, and then set aside only a small portion of our life, and tell him it is his.

When we become a Christian, we do not accept Christ, as though we made a choice to allow Christ to enter us. We are not the ones doing the choosing. God chose us. (John 6:37, 44, 65, 10:29, 15:16-19) While we were in our sin, Christ died for us. (Romans 5:6-8) Jesus sent his Spirit to reside within us. We are now his temple, his residence, his house. We now belong to him as his possession. He owns us; we do not own ourselves.

Now it is God who makes both us and you stand firm in Christ. He anointed us, **set his seal of ownership on us**, and put his Spirit in our hearts as a deposit, guaranteeing what is to come. 2 Corinthians 1:21-22 (NIV)

Jesus is Lord; we are not! (Romans 10:9, Philippians 2:9-11) To be a Christian is to belong to God. We are now under his ownership—exclusively! We are now his agents to bring forth his glory as he sees fit. We cannot love him and continue to compartmentalize our lives as though we are offering up a portion for him. We do not belong to ourselves any longer; we are all his.

Or **do you not know** that **your body** is the temple of the Holy Spirit who is in you, whom you have from God, and **you are not your own**? For **you were bought at a price**. Therefore **glorify God** with your body. 1 Corinthians 6:19-20 (NET)

Reflection Questions

Do you have wonderful feelings about God? Wonderful. God enjoys your feelings for him. Now, how is your everyday life consistent with your feelings toward him?

How have you identified your love for God by your compartmentalized identity and activities?

How have you professed love for God, yet lived for the opposite?

How does your love for the things of this world compete with your love for God? Think of money, possessions, career, addictions, titles, your time, or pleasures (sexual pleasures, food, entertainment, sports, hobbies).

How do you love others? How is your love for others a choice on your part to love Jesus?

Chapter 9

Obedience to Love

Why did Jesus come and die? There are several good answers to this question. Most would say that Jesus came to die for our sins. Correct, but why? So my sins would be forgiven. Correct, but why? My sins have to be forgiven so that I won't go to hell after I die. Correct, but if that is our only understanding, we have missed God's purposes completely. How about, Jesus died so that I would go to heaven instead of hell? Is that better? No; the Bible doesn't even say that we are going to heaven after we die, even though we state that as our eternal hope. Don't misunderstand me. There is a heaven. God is there, and those who die in Christ will be with God forever. But living for eternity in God's presence is not the same as being transported to someplace nice, like heaven. There is much more to eternal life than being transported from earth to heaven. In fact, if that is all we know, we do not understand eternal life.

So, how about, Jesus died so that our sins would be forgiven so that our relationship with God would be reconciled and restored. Now we are getting somewhere. But why? Why do we need a reconciled relationship? So that we can live with God forever. Yes, but that answer is far too incomplete. How about, so that we could have eternal life and live forever. That sounds good, but what does it mean to live? What does it mean to die? Is eternal life just a matter of living forever? What constitutes life? The life we live on earth is filled with sin and all of the consequences of sin: war, crime, rejection, divisions, lies, manipulation, distrust, hatred, unforgiveness, divorce, broken homes, addictions, depression, loneliness and the list goes on and on. What if we lived in this state, but we never died. We just lived with sin, in a sinful world, but no one ever died. We just went on in our struggles year after year, century after century—forever. Someone couldn't even commit suicide to escape this life. If we lived forever that way, would that be eternal life? Obviously not!

Now, what if we lived forever, but sin was removed? What if there were no offenses of any kind? What if no one ever took advantage of anyone else to their detriment? In other words, there would be no war, no crime, no distrust; there would be essentially no fear that someone would do me wrong. Would that bring eternal life? Well, we are getting closer, but we're not there yet.

If we look at the Ten Commandments, we see that, with the exception of remembering the Sabbath day and honoring our father and mother, the rest of the commands focus on the "thou shalt nots". Don't have idols. Don't take the Lord's name in vain. Don't commit adultery. Don't murder. Don't covet. Don't steal. Don't lie about others. Would that get us eternal life—if we all just stopped doing the things we shouldn't do? I don't think so! We would still be missing the key motivational ingredient of our hearts, and that is to love one another. Love fulfills the law. (Matthew 7:12, 22:35-39) Jesus came to fulfill the law. (Matthew 5:17-20) And how did he do that? He brought us the power to love. He put his own Spirit within us. Love is the fulfillment of the law. Paul compared the written law to the law of love.

> Let no debt remain outstanding, except the continuing debt to love one another, for **he who loves his fellowman has fulfilled the law**. The commandments, "Do not commit adultery," "Do not murder," "Do not steal," "Do not covet," and whatever other commandment there may be, are summed up in this one rule: "Love your neighbor as yourself." Love does no harm to its neighbor. Therefore **love is the fulfillment of the law**. Romans 13:8-10 (NIV)

Knowing God

In Chapter 6 we discussed loving God with our minds. We discussed knowing God and God knowing us. Knowing each other's thinking and walking together is very much a part of our love relationship with God. Amos 3:3 says, "How can two walk together unless they agree." There are two components in this relationship. The first is to agree; the second is to walk together. What is this walk with the Lord? I can read his word and understand his instructions and commands, but what is the walk together?

As we come to understand God, we begin to see the reality that "God is love". That is who he is. If we are to walk with him, we must also love others as he loves. And in so doing, we come to know his love. *Actually, when we love others, it is really God's love flowing through us to someone else. He loves through those who love him. And as we witness his love through us, we come to know him, for he is love.*

> Dear friends, let us love one another, because **love is from God**, and **everyone who loves has been born of God and knows God. The one who does not love does not know God, because God is love**. 1 John 4:7-8 (HCSB)

Jesus said that eternal life was to know God. (John 17:3) We come to know God and to experience eternal life when we love. Without love, we are without eternal life. Love is an action word. Love is the giving of the substance of my life so that someone else may have more life. This is how God loves us. We love God when we love others in the same way. Loving is the essence of God's life—eternal life.

> We know that **we have passed from death to life because we love our brothers. The one who does not love remains in death**. Everyone who hates his brother is a murderer, and you know that no murderer has eternal life residing in him.

This is how we have come to know love: He laid down His life for us. We should also lay down our lives for our brothers. If anyone has this world's goods and sees his brother in need but closes his eyes to his ⌊need⌋—how can God's love reside in him?

Little children, we must not love with word or speech, but with truth and action. 1 John 3:14-18 (HCSB)

We began this discussion by asking what it means to be saved and to have eternal life. It should be clear at this point that we are saved from a depraved life and enter into a life that is in harmony with God. God is love; so eternal life is the result of everyone living in love for one another. What a glorious existence—eternal life!

Commanded to Love

Jesus commanded us to love. Is that just another law that we must obey? Didn't Jesus come so that we would not be under the law, so that we would not be condemned? Isn't this just an exchange of one set of laws for one simple law, to love? Didn't Jesus die for us so that nothing would be required of us? Aren't we saved by faith, not by works? Yes, but saved from what? If we continue to sin, and if we fail to love, is it possible to obtain eternal life? Isn't that what we have been discussing? Can we have eternal life without love? Clearly not! Can we count on salvation without loving God? Jesus came to save us from our own sinful lives that are destroying us—destroying us as individuals and destroying us as a people. The key to our salvation is to become lovers—a people who love God and love one another with perfection. Then everything will be perfect, and we will be in paradise. *Without perfect love there is no paradise.*

Love is the overriding substance of the kingdom of heaven. Even now, our love for one another identifies us as those who belong to this eternal kingdom. Jesus commands us to love one another, and through our love, the world will know that we belong to Jesus.

A new command I give you: Love one another. As I have loved you, so you must love one another. **By this all men will know that you are my disciples, if you love one another**." John 13:34-35 (NIV)

And how do we love God? What if I say, "I love God because he sent his only Son to die for my sins." Is that love for God? Or is that just appreciation for how he loved us? What does it mean to love God? Jesus said,

If you love me, you will obey what I command. John 14:15 (NIV)

If you obey my commands, you will remain in my love, just as I have obeyed my Father's commands and remain in his love. I have told you this so that my joy may be in you and that your joy may be complete. **My command is this: Love each other as I have loved you**. John 15:10-12 (NIV)

To love Jesus is to do what he commands. He commands us to love others as he loved us. So, to love Jesus is to sacrificially love others. Notice in these words of our Lord that he gives the key for remaining in his love. We remain in his love by obeying his command to love one another.

For many, this may sound like heresy. Aren't we saved by faith, not by works? Why would I have to love others in order to be loved by Jesus? Didn't Jesus die for me while I still walked in sin? Doesn't he love me unconditionally?

But God demonstrates his own love for us in this: While we were still sinners, Christ died for us. Romans 5:8 (NIV)

Some might say, "Does this make sense? God loved me enough while I was a disobedient sinner to send his son to die for me so that my sins would be forgiven, but now Jesus says that he only loves me if I obey his command to love others as he loved me? What is the logic in this conclusion?" *Caution: Before we reject this understanding that our love is a requirement, remember, these are Jesus' words. Do we believe what he said or not?*

First, to answer these questions we must first hold tight to the words of Jesus. If our thinking does not line up with Jesus' words, we need to change our thinking. We need to search out God's word to make sense of any confusion or apparent contradictions. The truth is not found by holding tight to the verses that support our doctrines and to ignore those verses that contradict them. In the previous verses, Jesus clearly commands us to love, and without love we lose our connection with him. *Our salvation—our deliverance from the sin that is killing us—is found in obeying Jesus' command to love.*

Jesus came and died for our sins and then sent his Spirit to live within us so that we would have the love of God living within us. Remember, God is love. With his love living and flowing from us, we can pass from death to life—eternal life. *Salvation is not about being transported to some nice place. It is about being transformed into the likeness of God so that we live with his character by the Spirit he has given us.* (Galatians 5:22-25)

> We know that we have passed from death to life, because we love our brothers. Anyone who does not love remains in death. 1 John 3:14 (NIV)

We talk about being saved, but saved from what? We are saved from eternal death, which is total separation from God. God is life. In order to have God's life, we need to be connected to him so that his life will flow into and through us to others. God is love, and to have his life, his love must flow through us. *This is not legalistic salvation. This is the definition of eternal life. To have God's life is to have his love living in and through us. If we do not have love for others, we have lost our connection with God.* Jesus was very clear about this.

"I am the true vine and my Father is the gardener. He takes away every branch that does not bear fruit in me. He prunes every branch that bears fruit so that it will bear more fruit. You are clean already because of the word that I have spoken to you. **Remain in me, and I will remain in you. Just as the branch cannot bear fruit by itself, unless it remains in the vine, so neither can you unless you remain in me.**

"I am the vine; you are the branches. The one who remains in me—and I in him—bears much fruit, because apart from me you can accomplish nothing. If anyone does not remain in me, he is thrown out like a branch, and dries up; and such branches are gathered up and thrown into the fire, and are burned up.** If you remain in me and my words remain in you, ask whatever you want, and it will be done for you. My Father is honored by this, that you bear much fruit and show that you are my disciples.

"Just as the Father has loved me, I have also loved you; remain in my love. **If you obey my commandments, you will remain in my love**, just as I have obeyed my Father's commandments and remain in his love. I have told you these things so that my joy may be in you, and your joy may be complete. **My commandment is this—to love one another just as I have loved you. No one has greater love than this— that one lays down his life for his friends. You are my friends if you do what I command you.** I no longer call you slaves, because the slave does not understand what his master is doing. But I have called you friends, because I have revealed to you everything I heard from my Father. **You did not choose me, but I chose you and appointed you to go and bear fruit, fruit that remains,** so that whatever you ask the Father in my name he will give you. **This I command you—to love one another.** John 15:1-17 (NET)

These words of Jesus are filled with several <u>conditional</u> promises:

- If I remain in him, he will remain in me.
- If I remain in him, I will bear much fruit.
- If I do not remain in him and bear fruit, I will be cut off from Jesus and discarded to be burned.
- I can do nothing without being connected to Jesus, but I can do anything he commands if I remain connected to him.
- His command is to love. If I obey this command, I will remain in him.
- If I obey his command to love others, I will remain in his love for me.
- True joy is found in obeying his command to love others.
- I am his friend—if I obey his command to love others as he loved us.
- Jesus chose me to bear his fruit. I am commanded to love one another.
- If I obey Jesus' command to love, I can ask whatever I want of the Father and expect to receive it.

I suggest that you reread this passage again and witness for yourself these conditional promises found in Jesus' words to us. What he says is true. Now the ball is in our court. Will we believe what he clearly says, and will we follow him by obeying his commands?

Connected with Jesus

What do these words of Jesus say about our connection with Jesus? Love is our connection. I may pray, have faith, give my money, go to church and sing praises, but without love, these do nothing for my connection with Jesus. The Pharisees quoted the Scriptures, prayed often and exhibited many other religious activities, but they did not love—and they totally missed their connection with Jesus. In fact, they were jealous of his following, did not believe he was the Savior of the world, and they had him killed. They were religious, but they did not love others or Jesus. Prayer, faith, going to church and other religious disciplines are extremely important in our walk with Jesus, but without love for God and others, they are useless. *Anything that we might do, thinking that it is for and through God, is worthless without love.*

> If I speak in the tongues of men and of angels, but have not love, **I am only a resounding gong or a clanging cymbal**. If I have the gift of prophecy and can fathom all mysteries and all knowledge, and if I have a faith that can move mountains, but **have not love, I am nothing**. If I give all I possess to the poor and surrender my body to the flames, but have not love, **I gain nothing**. 1 Corinthians 13:1-3 (NIV)

How about God's word? Doesn't knowing and studying God's word connect me with Jesus? After all, Jesus is the word of God. Again, the Pharisees knew God's word. They were the guardians of his word. But because they did not love, they did not have a connection with Jesus. Look again at verse two; if I have "all knowledge—but have not love, I am nothing".

What about faith? Isn't faith our connection with Jesus? Aren't we saved by faith? Look again at verse two; "if I have a faith that can move mountains, but have not love, I am nothing". As important and essential as faith may be, without love, it is worthless. Our faith should be expressed in how we love. That is what counts. Without love, our faith is just a whitewash covering of an unregenerate heart that has no connection with Jesus.

> The only thing that counts is faith expressing itself through love. Galatians 5:6 (NIV)

Out of my love for others comes my prayer connection with Jesus. Out of love for others, my knowledge of his word comes alive. Out of love for others, my faith has substance; it is filled with Jesus Christ.

In fact, out of our love for others, we come to know the full extent of God's love for us. Out of love for others, we become filled with the full nature of God and his power. We will know his love beyond our mental understanding of his love. We will know his love because we will have seen it in action, firsthand, as he loves through us.

> For this reason I kneel before the Father, from whom every family in heaven and on the earth is named. I pray that according to the wealth of his glory he may grant you to be strengthened with power through his Spirit in the inner person, that Christ may dwell in your hearts through faith, so that, because **you have been rooted and grounded in love**, you may be able to comprehend with all the saints what is the breadth and length and height and depth, and thus to **know the love of Christ that surpasses knowledge, so that you may be filled up to all the fullness of God**. Ephesians 3:14-19 (NET)

This is the connection with Jesus that we all should be seeking. Ultimately, it is the only one that really matters.

Saved by His Spirit

This may all sound very legalistic if we do not understand that all that Jesus commands of us is empowered by his indwelling Spirit. It should be clear, as Jesus stated, unless we remain in him, we can do nothing. It is not that nothing is expected from us. Rather, everything is expected from us because we are now connected to him. It is his power and his will that is working in and through us. Jesus does his work through us by his word and his Spirit. Remember that he said we would bear much fruit—the fruit of his Spirit (Galatians 5:22-23)—if we remained in him through our obedience. He said that he chose us to bear much fruit, fruit that would last for eternity.

Jesus was sent to save us. He brought his life-giving word to us; Jesus is the word. (John 1:1, 14) He also sent his Spirit to live within us. By his Spirit and by his word we have a life-giving connection to Jesus. This is how he has saved us.

But we ought to thank God always for you, brothers and sisters loved by the Lord, because God chose you from the beginning for **salvation through sanctification by the Spirit and faith in the truth**. 2 Thessalonians 2:13 (NET)

But "when the kindness of God our Savior and his love for mankind appeared, **he saved us** not by works of righteousness that we have done but on the basis of his mercy, **through the washing of the new birth and the renewing of the Holy Spirit**, whom he poured out on us in full measure through Jesus Christ our Savior. And so, since we have been justified by his grace, we become heirs with the confident expectation of eternal life." Titus 3:4-7 (NET)

The one who sows to please his sinful nature, from that nature will reap destruction; **the one who sows to please the Spirit, from the Spirit will reap eternal life**. Galatians 6:8 (NIV)

Without the blood of Jesus, our relationship with God would not have been reconciled and restored. But without his word and his Spirit, it is impossible to have a relationship with God. After Jesus was raised from the dead and returned to his Father, he sent back the Holy Spirit to live within us. Living in obedience to his indwelling Spirit keeps us connected to Jesus. If we refuse to obey and to love, we lose our connection—and we lose the life that was freely paid for and provided for us.

Our life-giving connection with God is founded on having God's love flow in and through us as we love others with God's love. God is love; so all love originates with God and freely flows through us to others, but not if we lose the connection by disobedience.

Dear friends, let us love one another, for **love comes from God. Everyone who loves has been born of God and knows God. Whoever does not love does not know God, because God is love**. 1 John 4:7-8 (NIV)

No one has ever seen God; but **if we love one another, God lives in us and his love is made complete in us.** 1 John 4:12 (NIV)

And so we know and rely on the love God has for us. **God is love. Whoever lives in love lives in God, and God in him.** 1 John 4:16 (NIV)

We don't just automatically love. That is why Jesus talks about obeying his command to love one another. We have been freely given all that we need to love, but it requires of us to make the choice to obey Jesus' command to do it. There is competition living within us. Our old sinful nature is selfish and opposes sacrificial love. The sinful flesh and the Spirit are enemies. We are at the crossroads between these two opposing forces. It is our choice to put to death the ways of the sinful nature by the Spirit and to sow to the ways of the Spirit, which is to love. And when we do so, we reap eternal life.

The one who sows to please his sinful nature, from that nature will reap destruction; **the one who sows to please the Spirit, from the Spirit will reap eternal life.** Galatians 6:8 (NIV)

The entire law is summed up in a single command: "Love your neighbor as yourself". If you keep on biting and devouring each other, watch out or you will be destroyed by each other.

So I say, **live by the Spirit, and you will not gratify the desires of the sinful nature. For the sinful nature desires what is contrary to the Spirit, and the Spirit what is contrary to the sinful nature. They are in conflict with each other,** so that you do not do what you want. Galatians 5:14-17 (NIV)

If Jesus had not come and died for us and then rise from the dead, we would still be separated from God and lost without the living power of his transforming Spirit. But now we have the power of his life living right within us. The final outcome of this life is to live harmoniously with one another in perfect love for one another and God. Without love, there is no eternal life. This eternal life is not just living forever; it is living a life of love. Eternal life is a life of love. God is love. We now have his love living within us. But it takes obedience for this life to manifest.

Remember what Jesus said about our love for him and his love for us.

If you love me, you will obey what I command. John 14:15 (NIV)
If you obey my commands, you will remain in my love, just as I have obeyed my Father's commands and remain in his love. John 15:10 (NIV)
My command is this: Love each other as I have loved you. John 15:12 (NIV)

How do we love God? We love God by obeying his commands. And his primary and foundational command is to love one another as he loved us. When we are "born of God" we are saying that we are children of God. As children of God, together, we are of the same family of God. We are brothers and sisters of one another and Jesus. If we love our Father, we will love our brothers and sisters. This is love for God.

Everyone who believes that Jesus is the Christ has been born of God, and **everyone who loves the Father loves whoever has been born of him.** By this we know that we love the children of God, when we love God and obey his commandments. **For this is the love of God, that we keep his commandments.** And his commandments are not burdensome. For everyone who has been born of God overcomes the world. And this is the victory that has overcome the world—our faith. Who is it that overcomes the world except the one who believes that Jesus is the Son of God? 1 John 5:1-5 (ESV)

How Are We to Love One Another?

Love may have feelings, but Biblical love is an action. It is an action that makes a difference in another's life. Jesus commands us to love others as he loved us. (John 13:34, 15:12) Jesus gave up his life for us. He defines love, and he told us what the greatest love entails.

No one has greater love than this, that someone would lay down his life for his friends. John 15:13 (HCSB)

It is easy to say, "I love you." And these words can be very uplifting to someone. But if our love is mostly just words, it lacks the true substance of love. Biblical love is sacrificial. It is a giving of myself to someone else for their benefit.

Dear children, let us not love with words or tongue but with actions and in truth. 1 John 3:18 (NIV)

Our faith becomes real when it goes beyond our professions and exhibits itself in how we love others. Faith in action is seen in our love for others. And our love for others is seen when we give of our sustenance for the sake of others.

What good is it, my brothers, if someone says he has faith but does not have works? Can his faith save him? If a brother or sister is without clothes and lacks daily food and one of you says to them, "Go in peace, keep warm, and eat well," but you don't give them what the body needs, what good is it? In the same way **faith, if it doesn't have works, is dead by itself**. James 2:14-17 (HCSB)

Jesus was quite clear about how he will come at the end of time and how he will determine who are going to inherit eternal life and those who will be condemned to eternal punishment. He will separate them by how they loved him by loving other brothers and sisters in Christ. (Matthew 25:31-46) And how did they love him?

> For I was hungry and you gave me something to eat, I was thirsty and you gave me something to drink, I was a stranger and you invited me in, I needed clothes and you clothed me, I was sick and you looked after me, I was in prison and you came to visit me.' Matthew 25:35-36 (NIV)

Those who were identified as those who loved him in these ways received eternal life. Those who did not love like this went away to eternal punishment (Matthew 25:46).

> "Then he will say to those on his left, 'Depart from me, you cursed, into the eternal fire prepared for the devil and his angels. For I was hungry and you gave me no food, I was thirsty and you gave me no drink, I was a stranger and you did not welcome me, naked and you did not clothe me, sick and in prison and you did not visit me.' Then they also will answer, saying, 'Lord, when did we see you hungry or thirsty or a stranger or naked or sick or in prison, and did not minister to you?' Then he will answer them, saying, 'Truly, I say to you, **as you did not do it to one of the least of these, you did not do it to me**.' **And these will go away into eternal punishment, but the righteous into eternal life**." Matthew 25:41-46 (ESV)

We are commanded to love as Jesus loved us and gave his life for us. This is not legalistic salvation; loving one another is the substance of eternal life. Without it, we are still dead. As John wrote, we pass from death to life by loving our brothers and sisters in Christ.

> We know that we have passed from death to life, because we love our brothers. **Anyone who does not love remains in death**. Anyone who

hates his brother is a murderer, and you know that no murderer has eternal life in him. 1 John 3:14-15 (NIV)

And this life is seen in our giving up of our time, our possessions, our money, our service, our intellect and skills for the sake of someone else.

We have come to know love by this: that **Jesus laid down his life for us; thus we ought to lay down our lives for our fellow Christians**. But whoever has the world's possessions and sees his fellow Christian in need and shuts off his compassion against him, **how can the love of God reside in such a person?** 1 John 3:16-17 (NET)

This is love for God!!!

Reflection Questions

How have you been abiding in Jesus? Remember, that the reality of our abiding connection is realized by obeying his command to love others as he loved us.

Jesus commanded us to love one another as he loved us. For whom and how have you complied with this command?

How has loving been a difficult task for you? Name specific examples. When have you been challenged to love your "enemy"?

Forgiveness is love. Are you holding anyone in unforgiveness.

Chapter 10

Pleasing God

To please someone is to bring pleasure to them. Does it not make sense that to love someone, we would seek to bring them pleasure? Think of the love between a husband and wife. Love may be expressed with a gift, or giving each other time with devoted attention, or special words of endearment, encouragement or affirmation. It may be a backrub or enjoying a sexual encounter together. A marriage without seeking to please each other is dry and lacks love.

Think of the love for our children. We don't want to spoil our children, but if we are not blessing them in tangible ways that bring them pleasure, they will not sense that they are loved. A father may take his son fishing or to play ball. A mother may make a cake to celebrate her child's birthday. Parents teach, encourage, train and value their children, and their children derive great pleasure in knowing that they are valued. Loving parents spend time with their children and engage in their lives. They also invite their children to be part of their lives. The list goes on in many and varied directions, but a child knows he is loved when he sees his parents seeking to bring blessings into his life.

To love is to look out for the interests of others. (Philippians 2:4) To love is to be a blessing to others. We are to bless our enemies, how much more our loved ones. (1 Peter 3:9) Our opportunities to bless others and to bring pleasure into their lives are all around us every day. To love is to bless and to bring pleasure to another. Jesus said that we are more blessed when we become a blessing to others. (Acts 20:35)

If this is how we communicate and act out our love for others, should we not also love God in the same way?

And how do we do that—bring pleasure to God? Paul said we are to "find out what pleases the Lord". Ephesians 5:10 (NIV)

A child has the opportunity to bring pleasure to his father or mother—a pleasure that only the child can bring. How can we give God something that he cannot easily provide for himself? If we look to the Scriptures, we find many ways that we can bring pleasure to God. Let's take a look at a few that are fundamental for all of us.

God's Pleasure from Our Faith

We read in Hebrews that "without faith it is impossible to please God".

By faith Enoch was taken away so he did not experience death, and he was not to be found because God took him away. For prior to his removal he was approved, **since he had pleased God**. Now **without faith it is impossible to please God**, for the one who draws near to Him must believe that He exists and rewards those who seek Him. Hebrews 11:5-6 (HCSB)

If we are to please God—if we are to love him—we must walk in faith. So what does it mean to have faith? What is the difference between believing God and having faith in God? Prior to the verse just quoted we have a definition of faith.

Now faith is being sure of what we hope for, being convinced of what we do not see. Hebrews 11:1 (NET)

This is a commonly quoted verse, but by itself, we still do not have a grasp of faith in God. Let me give an illustration of belief versus faith. There was a tightrope walker who had a cable stretched across Niagara Falls. He had a wheelbarrow which he pushed back and forth on this tightrope. Soon a large crowd formed to witness this frightful feat. After several passes, he addressed the crowd, "Who *believes* that I can go back and forth again?" To which, every hand went up. Then he asked them another question, "Who will get in the wheel barrow and go with me?" To which every hand went down. They all believed, but none would trust their lives to his ability to safely cross on the tightrope above the falls.

Faith is not only believing, but faith is trusting God with our lives. It is obeying him in frightful and difficult situations because we trust his power, his wisdom and his love for us. It is seeking his ways and his will for our lives because he is God Almighty. It is acknowledging that we are his possessions in that we obey his commands. Faith is seeking out his promises and then living out our lives, believing in and depending upon his promises.

Chapter 11 of Hebrews gives a long list of examples of men and women of faith, but let's just look at Abraham. Abraham is called the father of our faith. Abraham lived in Haran with his family—his father and all of his relatives. At seventy-five years old God told him to leave his father, mother and relatives and head out to Canaan. He promised him that he would bless him by making his name great and that he would be the father of a great nation. So he trusted God and left his family home. He left his loved ones and his place of security out of obedience to God's commands—not knowing exactly where he would settle, how God would fulfill his promises to him or when. He just obediently went. He trusted God. He believed him and he acted upon his beliefs. He had faith in God.

By faith Abraham, when he was called, obeyed and went out to a place he was going to receive as an inheritance. He went out, not knowing where he was going. **By faith** he stayed as a foreigner in the land of promise, living in tents with Isaac and Jacob, coheirs of the same promise. For he was looking forward to the city that has foundations, whose architect and builder is God. Hebrews 11:8-10 (HCSB)

God had promised to make a great nation out of Abraham's offspring, but his wife Sarah could not get pregnant. Abraham's faith was being tested. Abraham was now one hundred and his wife was ninety. Abraham had waited twenty-five years for God to fulfill his promise to him, and now it looked like it was way too late. But Abraham stilled looked to God to fulfill his word.

> By faith even Sarah herself, when she was unable to have children, received power to conceive offspring, even though she was past the age, since she considered that the One who had promised was faithful. Therefore from one man—in fact, from one as good as dead—came offspring as numerous as the stars of heaven and as innumerable as the grains of sand by the seashore. Hebrews 11:11-12 (HCSB)

Abraham had just one son, Isaac, by his wife Sarah. He was the miracle child given to them. He was the only means of fulfilling the promise God made to Abraham to multiply his offspring into a great nation. And then one day, when his son Isaac was just a boy, God came to Abraham and told him to take his son up on a mountain and sacrifice him there on an altar to God. Abraham obeyed. He trusted God, even though he was being told to kill his only son; even though this son was the only means of fulfilling God's promise to Abraham. He went up the mountain, tied up his son on an altar, and raised his knife to stab him to death. And just at that moment, an angel stopped him. God provided a ram to slay in his son's place. Isaac was spared, but not without the test of Abraham's faith. Abraham pleased God!

> By faith Abraham, when he was tested, offered up Isaac. He received the promises and he was offering his unique son, the one it had been said about, Your seed will be traced through Isaac. He considered God to be able even to raise someone from the dead, and as an illustration, he received him back. Hebrews 11:17-19 (HCSB)

It should be clear from just these examples of Abraham's faith that faith is much more than just believing. Faith requires action to prove itself. Faith is believing what God says, and then living our lives in concert with our beliefs. Faith is choosing to obey God's commands instead of choosing to fulfill our own desires. Our choice to do things God's way is out of our trust in God, but much more. If God is not the Lord of our lives, how can we act in faith? Faith requires of us to do what he says, first because he is Lord, second because God's ways are always right, and thirdly because he is trustworthy. This is love for God. This is what it means to walk in faith. James put it very succinctly.

> What good is it, my brothers, if someone says he has faith but does not have works? Can his faith save him?
>
> If a brother or sister is without clothes and lacks daily food and one of you says to them, "Go in peace, keep warm, and eat well," but you don't give them what the body needs, what good is it? In the same way **faith, if it doesn't have works, is dead by itself**.
>
> But someone will say, "You have faith, and I have works." Show me your faith without works, and **I will show you faith from my works**. You believe that God is one; you do well. The demons also believe—and they shudder.
>
> Foolish man! Are you willing to learn that faith without works is useless? Wasn't Abraham our father justified by works when he offered Isaac his son on the altar? You see that **faith was active together with his works, and by works, faith was perfected**. So the Scripture was fulfilled that says, Abraham believed God, and it was credited to him for righteousness, and he was called God's friend. You see that a man is justified by works and not by faith alone. James 2:14-24 (HCSB)

Our lives are filled with choices that direct our behaviors. It does not matter whether or not someone believes in God or not, his whole life is a continuum of choices. How do we make these choices? Choices are driven by our hearts and minds—we decide. Without being born again of the Spirit of Christ, the only spirit driving our choices is that of our old nature, the sinful nature. The sinful nature is driven to please our own self before pleasing others. So our choices are based on being the lord of our own lives. Without the Spirit living within us, the choices we make are made out of our own wisdom, which is faulty and will likely lead us down a wrong path. We put our trust in our own strengths, abilities and thinking, which have minute power compared to God's infinite power. We all have to make daily choices, minute-by-minute, and situation-by-situation. We cannot escape having to make life choices. To have faith in God is to make these choices based on God's will, God's wisdom and God's power to control the details of life now and out into the distant future. Faith consists of believing that God should be the one we follow rather than our own will. Faith is believing God and then living accordingly with our life choices. Saying that we have faith in God and then living according to our own will, contrary to his will, is a lie.

It pleases God when we, in faith, seek his wisdom for our lives and obediently trust him with our lives. *Faith is trusting God with our lives, and that requires making numerous choices and actions in our lives based on his will and wisdom.* This is faith. This is what pleases God. This is love for God. The Psalmist put it this way.

Let the morning bring me word of your unfailing love, for **I have put my trust in you. Show me the way I should go, for to you I lift up my soul**. Rescue me from my enemies, O LORD, for **I hide myself in you. Teach me to do your will, for you are my God; may your good Spirit lead me on level ground**. For your name's sake, O LORD, preserve my life; in your righteousness, bring me out of trouble. In your unfailing love, silence my enemies; destroy all my foes, for I am your servant. Psalm 143:8-12 (NIV)

Either God is in control of our lives by our faith in God or our sinful nature is in control. God is pleased when our faith in him controls. It displeases God when our sinful nature is in control.

Those controlled by the sinful nature cannot please God. Romans 8:8 (NIV)

Pride is at the center of the sinful nature. Pride is thinking that we are self-sufficient. Pride is a mental state of being independent of God. This is the essence of the fall of Adam and Eve, the choice to live life apart from God with the thinking that we are capable and better off for doing so. God finds no pleasure in the prideful. In fact, he abhors them.

Everyone with **a proud heart is detestable to the LORD**; be assured, he will not go unpunished. Proverbs 16:5 (HCSB)

Pride is thinking that we are more than what we actually are. It is living out a lie about ourselves. Humility is living a truthful life, knowing that we are weak and dependent beings under the care of our Almighty God. God opposes the proud, but gives grace to the humble.

In the same way, you younger men, be subject to the elders. And all of you **clothe yourselves with humility** toward one another, because **"God resists the proud but gives grace to the humble"** [Proverbs 3:34]. Humble yourselves, therefore, under the mighty hand of God, so that He may exalt you at the proper time, casting all your care on Him, because He cares about you. 1 Peter 5:5-7 (HCSB)

The proud cannot please God. He finds no pleasure in them. But he finds great delight in those who fear him and live their lives, knowing that everything depends upon God. He is the creator of all things, and all things hold together through Jesus. (Colossians 1:15-17) The man who lives his life dependent upon God's might and love brings great pleasure to God. He finds no pleasure in those who think they are sufficient in their own minute strengths.

> **His pleasure is not** in the strength of the horse, **nor his delight in** the legs of a man; **the LORD delights in those who fear him, who put their hope in his unfailing love**. Psalm 147:10-11 (NIV)

True Worship

We talk a lot today about worshipping God. From my observation, we have narrowed worship down to singing songs to God in a church service. Singing songs to God may be worship, but only if our hearts are set on pleasing God in faith. True worship to God requires our faith in him. True worship requires giving our lives to him in how we think, our attitudes, our choices and behaviors. Paul put it this way.

> Therefore, brothers, by the mercies of God, I urge you to present your bodies as a living sacrifice, holy and **pleasing to God**; **this is your spiritual worship**. Do not be conformed to this age, but be transformed by the renewing of your mind, so that you may discern what is the good, **pleasing**, and perfect will of God. Romans 12:1-2 (HCSB)

The Pharisees were big talkers, but they did not know God; they did not love God or obey God's commands. Instead, they made up their own traditions and called them worship, but their worship was in vain. What they said with their words did not match up with their lives. Jesus quoted Isaiah against them.

> These people honor Me with their lips, but their heart is far from Me. They worship Me in vain, teaching as doctrines the commands of men." Matthew 15:*8-9 (HCSB) [from Isaiah 29:13]*

Here is the key to true worship. If we really love God, we will love his ways of living. We will love his ways of thinking. We will love the nature of his kingdom and his Spirit. We will love his truth about our lives and life eternal. We will want all that he has for us and be willing to give up anything to obtain it. We will sow to his Spirit and bear the fruit of his Spirit in our daily lives. That is what it means when we say we love God. It is hypocrisy to express all sorts of lovely devotions to God, and then go on with our lives in the same old fashion as before. Living for the pleasures and satisfactions of our fleshly nature and the world is contrary to love for God. And the one who lives like this cannot truly worship God, no matter what he says or how he feels when singing songs to him. God is looking for reality in our worship, not a momentary experience.

Ezekiel was confronted with a people who delighted in music and songs of praise, but their hearts were cold to God as evidenced in their lack of applying what they heard to their lives.

My people come to you, as they usually do, and sit before you to listen to your words, but **they do not put them into practice**. **With their mouths they express devotion**, **but their hearts are greedy** for unjust gain. Indeed, to them you are nothing more than one who sings love songs with a beautiful voice and plays an instrument well, for **they hear your words but do not put them into practice**. Ezekiel 33:31-32 (NIV)

As Paul wrote to the Romans (earlier passage), true worship is the offering of our bodily lives to God for his purposes, and this true worship pleases God. True worship requires much more than what we say and how we sing; it requires living for God in our daily lives.

Pleasing God with How We Live

If we truly love someone—say our spouse—don't we intentionally do things that we know will please them, things that will bring them pleasure. Maybe they cherish a hug. Maybe they are in need of words of encouragement, or just someone to listen as they pour out the things of their heart. Or maybe they have a physical need where you could serve them. Maybe they would be elated by a surprise gift—maybe a bouquet of flowers. If we love someone, we will seek to do the things that please them.

If we love God, we need to know what pleases him and then do what pleases him. So what pleases God? We have already discussed our acting out in faith and the worship of God with our lives. But let's be more specific. What specific actions on our part please God? What does Scripture tells us?

Jesus came proclaiming the good news of his kingdom. At one point he said that this was the reason that he was sent. (Luke 4:43) When asked how to pray, he told us to pray, "Your kingdom come. Your will be done on earth as it is in heaven." (Matthew 6:10) He told us to seek his kingdom and righteousness as a first priority in our lives. (Matthew 6:33) Paul wrote that living for the kingdom is pleasing to God. So it should be clear that if we are to seek God's pleasure, we should seek to know God's kingdom so that we can live for his kingdom. This is pleasing to God.

For the kingdom of God is not a matter of eating and drinking, but of **righteousness, peace and joy in the Holy Spirit,** because **anyone who serves Christ in this way is pleasing to God** and approved by men. Romans 14:17-18 (NIV)

"Anyone who serves Christ in this way is pleasing to God". What do we know about serving Christ in his kingdom? Kingdom is mentioned 160 times in the New Testament. "Kingdom of God" or "kingdom of heaven" are mentioned 98 times. Jesus refers to his kingdom 35 times in the book of Matthew alone. After Jesus' resurrection he spent forty days speaking about matters concerning the kingdom of God before ascending into heaven. (Acts 1:3) At the last Passover supper, Jesus said that he would not drink of the fruit of the vine again until he drinks it anew in his Father's kingdom. (Luke 22:18) Paul spent three months at Ephesus synagogue persuasively arguing about the kingdom of God. (Acts 19:8) One day at Rome Paul taught about this kingdom from morning to evening. (Acts 2:23) Kingdoms and the conflict between God's kingdom and the kingdom of darkness is a theme throughout the Bible. Our eternal existence with be in the kingdom of God. (Revelation 11:15, 12:10, 2 Peter 1:10-11) How much do we know about this eternal kingdom, this heavenly kingdom, the kingdom of God? To please God we need to study God's word to understand it so that we can seek it and live for it. Jesus said that the kingdom of God was within and among us. (Luke 17:20-21) Are we even aware of this heavenly kingdom? We live on this earth in the kingdom of darkness. Are we exhibiting the kingdom of light, shining forth the glory of God? (Colossians 1:12-13) If we love God, we should all be seeking to reveal his kingdom in who we are and how we live. There should be a stark difference between God's children and the children of this world. Many proclaim to be Christians, but are they Christ followers? Jesus is the King of his kingdom. Are we serving our Lord and King such that others would know where our citizenship lies?

Living according to God's Spirit is pleasing to God. This means that we must be sensitive to the leading of his Spirit within us, and then follow this leading. Our sinful nature is always speaking and attempting to influence our thinking, attitude and behavior. It pleases God to focus on the Spirit's leading and to live in such a manner that we exhibit the character of God in our daily lives.

This endeavor requires of us to seek God's will so that we can walk in it. It requires that we invest ourselves in God's word so that we can live according to his ways and will. Then it requires to obediently bear the fruit of his Spirit, now that we know how we are supposed to think and act. This way of living is pleasing to God. It is how we love him.

And so, from the day we heard, we have not ceased to pray for you, asking that you may be **filled with the knowledge of his will in all spiritual wisdom and understanding**, so as to **walk in a manner**

worthy of the Lord, fully pleasing to him, bearing fruit in every good work and increasing in the knowledge of God. Colossians 1:9-10 (ESV)

Finally, brothers, we instructed you **how to live in order to please God**, as in fact you are living. Now we ask you and urge you in the Lord Jesus to do this more and more. 1 Thessalonians 4:1 (NIV)

I urge, then, first of all, that requests, prayers, intercession and thanksgiving be made for everyone—for kings and all those in authority, that we may live peaceful and quiet lives in all godliness and holiness. **This is good, and pleases God our Savior**, who wants all men to be saved and to come to a knowledge of the truth. 1 Timothy 2:1-4 (NIV)

Specifically, we please God when we sacrificially live for others. Without love for others, it is impossible to please God. And it is impossible to love God, for God is love. Looking after widows, orphans and anyone who is in need is love for God and pleases him.

Honor widows who are truly in need. But if a widow has children or grandchildren, they should first learn to fulfill their duty toward their own household and so repay their parents what is owed them. **For this is what pleases God**. 1 Timothy 5:3-4 (NET)

Do not neglect to do good and to share what you have, for **such sacrifices are pleasing to God**. Hebrews 13:16 (ESV)

Religion that God our Father accepts as pure and faultless is this: to look after orphans and widows in their distress and to keep oneself from being polluted by the world. James 1:27 (NIV)

Like any father, God takes delight in his children. If we are to please God, we should work toward being delightful children.

For **the LORD takes delight in his people**; he crowns the humble with salvation. Psalm 149:4 (NIV)

This should not be that difficult to understand. Most of us have children. Sometimes they are not so delightful. We may still love them and do what is good and right for them. The exercise of good character, good behavior and good attitudes makes for delightful children. Rebellion, temper tantrums, complaining, disobedience, selfishness and the like are not delightful. What kind of children are we for God? Do we bring him delightful pleasure? Do we truly love him? Do we intentionally seek to please him?

The Faith of a Child

We look at ourselves, and we see ourselves as adults. Most of us have been married and have children of our own. So it is difficult to view ourselves as children—children of our heavenly Father. That is how God views us, as his children. And that is how we should view ourselves.

Think of the pleasure that we gain from our own children. There is a special joy that comes at every age—the tender little baby, the adorable one to two year old as they begin to crawl, walk and talk. We enjoy each year as they grow and learn and mature. From babies, to toddlers, to young children, preteens to teenagers, and then to see them become mature adults—there is joy at every stage. There are so many things that I enjoy doing with little kids that I may not enjoy by myself as an adult. Everything is new to them, and their reactions are fresh and innocent. When they are excited to do something, I partake in their excitement. Teaching them to ride a bike for the first time brings me great pleasure. I look forward toward taking them to catch their first fish. Just playing a game with them and letting them think they won brings joy and pleasure to me. And this is especially true for my own children. I cherish them and derive great joy from them. Teaching and training to see them progress in life brings forth a great pleasurable reward.

The Scriptures tell us that God disciplines us out of his love for us because out of the discipline we become more like him in true righteousness and holiness. (Hebrews 12:4-11) It has been said that a father endures more pain than his child when he invokes discipline. It hurts to see our loved ones go down the wrong road, but it gives us great pleasure to see them walking down the right road of life.

Children are not perfect. In fact, from birth they are selfish sinners. (Psalm 51:5, 58:3) We don't have to teach them to throw a temper tantrum, to lie or to be selfish. Instead, we have to teach them to submit, to tell the truth and to love others. But even knowing that they possess a sinful nature from birth, like us all, we still love them and find great pleasure in them. They are a treasure to us!

If we could only realize that our heavenly Father finds great joy and pleasure in us. Obviously, we are not all that we will be some day. We are just growing children in his sight. But he enjoys us. Like the two year old, we are still selfish and may even throw our adult temper tantrums, but he still loves us as our Father. And we are his children. We are his treasured possession.

Our heavenly Father takes great pleasure in us. He delights in our dependence upon him as our almighty and loving Father. He does not take delight in our prideful independence. The fear of the Lord comes from the understanding of our total dependence upon him for protection, provision, truth, anything good—for life itself. And all that we receive from him flows from his endless love for his children. Walking in the hope of his unfailing love brings God great delight to him, our loving heavenly Father.

His pleasure is not in the strength of the horse, nor **his delight** in the legs of a man; **the LORD delights** in those who fear him, who put their hope in his unfailing love. Psalm 147:10-11 (NIV)

A loved child looks up to his father and wants to be like him. He mimics him in many of his behaviors. Little boys always want to put on their dad's big boots and wear his huge work gloves. As the saying goes, "Like father, like son".

And what little child worries about tomorrow or what he will eat or wear or where he will sleep? Children rest in the care of their father. Life is a joy because they are covered by the provision and protection of Dad. That is how our heavenly Dad desires for us to live in his loving and all-powerful care. We are his children, and we bring him an abundance of pleasure.

We bring our heavenly Father great pleasure when we live as a child in his presence. Faith is a measure of our trust in him as our Father. Faith allows us not to worry about tomorrow. Faith allows us to seek him for wisdom and understanding. Faith allows us to rest in Him as a child rests in his earthly father. Faith gives us the power to know God and his love for us.

When we live our lives apart from God, looking to our own strengths and abilities as our first recourse or endeavor, we are not walking in the faith of a child. Look at whom Jesus raised up as having the greatest faith in the kingdom of God.

> At that time the disciples came to Jesus saying, "Who is the greatest in the kingdom of heaven?" He called a child, had him stand among them, and said, "I tell you the truth, **unless you turn around and become like little children**, you will never enter the kingdom of heaven! Whoever then humbles himself like this little child is the greatest in the kingdom of heaven. And whoever welcomes a child like this in my name welcomes me. Matthew 18:1-5 (NET)

Did you hear that? Unless we repent from acting like adults and become like little children in our relationship with God, we will never enter the kingdom of God. We are saved by faith, and faith requires of us to have a child-to-father relationship with God. Walking in self-sufficiency is not humbling ourselves as little children who love and trust their Father for all of life's needs.

This was not the only time that Jesus made such strong statements about receiving the kingdom of God as a little child.

> Now they were bringing even infants to him that he might touch them. And when the disciples saw it, they rebuked them. But Jesus called them to him, saying, "Let the children come to me, and do not hinder them, for to such belongs the kingdom of God. Truly, I say to you, whoever does not receive the kingdom of God like a child shall not enter it." Luke 18:15-17 (ESV)

Most churches segregate by ages: nursery, toddlers, grade levels, youth and adults. Adults do not think that there is much to gain from little children regarding faith, knowledge, wisdom and understanding. Notice that the disciples rebuked those who brought their children to Jesus. Jesus, in turn, rebuked his disciples. He didn't say to just put up with them out of love for them. He said that the kingdom of God belonged to the infants and children. He said that "whoever does not receive the kingdom of God like a child shall not enter it." Little children are precious to God. They bring him great pleasure. They may have a sinful nature, but they naturally trust in and depend on those who are older and much more capable. Their nature is to put their faith—their lives—in the hands of their parents. We could learn a great lesson from them. Do we have the faith of a child? Do we give God great pleasure because we look up to him for our needs—for life itself? Do we seek to be like our Father from our hearts? This is what children of God are like. Are we acting like children of God?

Reflection Questions

How has your faith pleased God? When have you deliberately chosen to do something because you believed it was God's will and you trusted him with your life in how you acted? Specifically, what did you do in faith, trusting in God?

What is your discipline to renew and transform your thinking so that you think and act in alignment with God's will?

How are you seeking God's kingdom and righteousness in your life? Describe his kingdom that you are pursuing.

Do you witness God's pleasure in you? Are you and your life pleasing to God?

How is your relationship with God as a little child? Or do you interact mostly as an adult who has left home to venture out on your own?

Chapter 11

Living for God's Purposes

Jesus prayed in the garden of Gethsemane at the Mount of Olives the night of his betrayal. He was in extreme agony, suffering for the sins of the world. Of course he did not want to suffer, but he knew that his life here on earth was not for his earthly will, but for the will of his Father in heaven.

Going a little farther, He fell facedown and prayed, "My Father! If it is possible, let this cup pass from Me. **Yet not as I will, but as You will**." Matthew 26:39 (HCSB)

Again, a second time, He went away and prayed, "My Father, if this cannot pass unless I drink it, **Your will be done**." Matthew 26:42 (HCSB)

"Father, **if you are willing, take this cup from me; yet not my will, but yours be done**." Luke 22:42 (NIV)

Jesus did not come on his own accord. He came because his Father sent him. And his Father sent him with a purpose. Jesus' entire life was lived to accomplish his Father's purposes. Jesus continually looked to his Father to know his Father's business, and then worked to accomplish his will. He was on assignment by his Father, and he was quite clear about it.

For I have come down from heaven, not to do my own will but the will of him who sent me. John 6:38 (ESV)

I can do nothing on my own. As I hear, I judge, and my judgment is just, because **I seek not my own will but the will of him who sent me**. John 5:30 (ESV)

Jesus always looked to his Father's directives in order to fulfill his Father's will and purpose. Jesus spent hours in prayer, and much of this time was for the purpose of knowing his Father's will so that he could accomplish his Father's purpose.

So Jesus answered them, "I tell you the solemn truth, the Son can do nothing on his own initiative, but only what he sees the Father doing. **For whatever the Father does, the Son does likewise**. For the Father loves the Son and shows him everything he does, and will show him greater deeds than these, so that you will be amazed. John 5:19-20 (NET)

For I did not speak of my own accord, but the Father who sent me **commanded me what to say and how to say it**. I know that his command leads to eternal life. **So whatever I say is just what the Father has told me to say.**" John 12:49-50 (NIV)

But the testimony that I have is greater than that of John. For **the works that the Father has given me to accomplish**, the very works that I am doing, bear witness about me that the Father has sent me. John 5:36 (ESV)

Fulfilling Jesus' Calling

Did Peter love Jesus? Think about it. Peter had a wife and a career. He was a fisherman by trade. That is how he supported himself and his family. One day he was at work fishing, and Jesus came along. Jesus called out to Peter to leave his fishing and follow Jesus in his "fishing" business. And Peter immediately left his trade to enter into Jesus' work.

> As Jesus was walking beside the Sea of Galilee, he saw two brothers, Simon called Peter and his brother Andrew. They were casting a net into the lake, for they were fishermen. **"Come, follow me," Jesus said, "and I will make you fishers of men." At once they left their nets and followed him.** Matthew 4:18-20 (NIV)

Did Peter love Jesus? He certainly appeared to. But let's flash forward three years. At this point Jesus is no longer a stranger to him, and he knows that Jesus is the foretold messiah who had come to reign. (Matthew 16:13-17) But Peter wasn't ready for Jesus being taken captive and crucified on a cross. On that night Peter denied even knowing Jesus three times. So now how much did he love Jesus?

Peter's relationship with Jesus began when he was called away from his fishing career. And now that Jesus had died and was risen, Peter went back to his fishing. Again, Jesus, now raised from dead, came to him as he was out fishing. And like before, he called him to follow by fulfilling Jesus' purposes, not his own.

And like his first calling, Peter had been out fishing all night and caught nothing. And like before, Jesus told them to put down their nets again, and the net became full of fish. Jesus told Peter to bring some of the fish to shore. And then Jesus challenged Peter with his love for him compared to the love of his own life and the love of working to catch these fish that they were looking at. Remember, Jesus first called Peter by telling him that he would make him a "fisher of men". (Matthew 4:19) And remember, Peter had denied Jesus three times to save his own life. And now Jesus asked him three times if he loved him more than his fishing career, because this time he was calling him, not only give up his fishing career for him, but to give up his life.

In the following setting, remember that are at the shore, finishing a breakfast of bread and fish. Peter had just dragged in his net of fish, and they are looking down at his large catch.

When they had finished breakfast, Jesus said to Simon Peter, "Simon, son of John, **do you love me more than these?**" He said to him, "Yes, Lord; you know that I love you." He said to him, **"Feed my lambs."** He said to him a second time, "Simon, son of John, **do you love me?**" He said to him, "Yes, Lord; you know that I love you." He said to him, **"Tend my sheep."** He said to him the third time, "Simon, son of John, **do you love me?**" Peter was grieved because he said to him the third time, "Do you love me?" and he said to him, "Lord, you know everything; you know that I love you." Jesus said to him, **"Feed my sheep**. Truly, truly, I say to you, when you were young, you used to dress yourself and walk wherever you wanted, but when you are old, you will stretch out your hands, and another will dress you and carry you where you do not want to go." (This he said to show by what kind of death he was to glorify God.) And after saying this he said to him, **"Follow me."** John 21:15-19 (ESV)

Jesus had called Peter to work for him fulltime. He called him to not only "fish for men", but to disciple them as he had been discipled. (Matthew 28:18-20) To "feed his lambs" was to nurture the young Christians. To "feed his sheep" was to bring them to maturity—to parent them. To "tend his sheep" was to unite them as a flock into a living body. (Ephesians 4:11-16) And after he had served Jesus in this manner, Jesus told him that he was going to lose his life as Jesus had lost his life. Remember, this was all in the context of "Do you love me?"

Jesus asks us the same; do we love him? Our calling will not be the same as Peter's calling. That should not matter. We need to answer the question: If he calls me, will I go? Will I give up the consistency of my life in order to fulfill what Jesus wants? Will we be like the prophet Isaiah when God asked, "Who should I send?"

Then I heard the voice of the Lord saying: Who should I send? Who will go for Us? I said: **Here I am. Send me.** Isaiah 6:8 (HCSB)

We cannot separate our love for God from the calling that he has upon our lives. To love God is to live our lives according to his purposes at the cost of giving up our own purposes.

And we know that for **those who love God** all things work together for good, for those who are **called according to his purpose.** Romans 8:28 (ESV)

Loving God can be very costly. Oh, we gain all that Jesus has—life eternal. We inherit his kingdom. We will reign with him for eternity. But if we want to be his disciples, we have to renounce our own ambitions for our lives and succumb to his will and purposes for us.

"If anyone comes to me and does not hate his father and mother, his wife and children, his brothers and sisters—**yes, even his own life**—he cannot be my disciple. **And anyone who does not carry his cross and follow me cannot be my disciple.**

"Suppose one of you wants to build a tower. Will he not first sit down and estimate the cost to see if he has enough money to complete it? For if he lays the foundation and is not able to finish it, everyone who sees it will ridicule him, saying, 'This fellow began to build and was not able to finish.'

"Or suppose a king is about to go to war against another king. Will he not first sit down and consider whether he is able with ten thousand men to oppose the one coming against him with twenty thousand? If he is not able, he will send a delegation while the other is still a long way off and will ask for terms of peace. **In the same way, any of you who does not give up everything he has cannot be my disciple.** Luke 14:26-33 (NIV)

Fulfilling God's Purposes Through Us

Jesus was about his Father's business, and now it is our turn. As Jesus was on assignment, so we are on assignment by God. As Jesus always looked to his Father to seek his will and his purposes, so should we as we serve Jesus. That is why we call Jesus Lord and Master. Why else would we give him these titles if we did not have it in mind to seek him for his will in our lives? As Jesus lived for the will of his Father, we now serve Jesus, but we are really serving the same will of the Father because that is the complete will of Jesus, to fulfill the Father's purposes. We belong to Jesus now, and we now have been appointed to carry out his business. We are his body at work. Jesus clearly calls us to his work. And like Peter, we are asked, "Do you love me?"

> You are my friends **if you do what I command**. I no longer call you servants, because a servant does not know his **master's business**. Instead, I have called you friends, **for everything that I learned from my Father I have made known to you.** You did not choose me, but **I chose you and appointed you to go and bear fruit**—fruit that will last. **Then the Father will give you whatever you ask in my name**. This is my command: Love each other. John 15:14-17 (NIV)

Look at the strong statements in this passage. Who is a friend of Jesus? Those who do what he commands of them. And when we do what he commands, we become intimately aware of our master's business. We are his business partners. This is not because we are affiliated with Jesus' name, but because we are about the Father's business here on earth. We are Jesus' agents to bring glory to the Father. Jesus is our Master and we seek him out to accomplish his will and purposes, which come from the

Father. We have been appointed by Jesus for this marvelous work, but it is work, the works of God. And as his agents—his workers—his business partners—and because we are living to accomplish his will as his servants, he promises to give us whatever we need to do his will. All we have to do is to ask the Father in Jesus' name. It is like the Father owns the business. Jesus is the Father's CEO, the Chief Executive Officer. And we are Jesus' managers. The resources are unlimited, so when we need anything to accomplish the will and purposes of the Father's business, he will make sure that we get what we need. The output of his business is to bear the fruit of his Spirit, whom he has given us. And the fruit of his Spirit is the foundation for the establishment of his kingdom. That is his ultimate purpose, to establish his kingdom. That is why when asked how we are to pray, Jesus instructed us to pray to our Father, "Your kingdom come. Your will be done on earth as it is in heaven." That is why he instructed us to seek his kingdom and his righteousness first in our life pursuits. (Matthew 6:33) We are to live to bring forth the Father's glory. His assignments will be different for each of us, so we need to be seeking him daily to know his specific will for us, as Jesus had done.

The devil has a kingdom as well. This world is his reign. (Matthew 4:8-9) And the foundation of his kingdom is self—to serve self above others. It is the opposite of love, which is to serve others above ourselves. An entire book could be written on the comparisons. But it should be obvious that the kingdom of God will be founded on loving one another, as compared to this world that is founded on serving our selves, much of the time at the cost of others. That is why Jesus said that he appointed us to love one another, to bear fruit for the Father's glory. Without love for one another, there is no life. God is love. (1 John 4:4, 16) Jesus is life—eternal life. (1 John 5:11, 20, 1:2, 11:25) Life among us proceeds from having God among us. God is love, so we are to live in love. Jesus is all truth; so to have his life, we must live in love and truth. These are foundational elements to the establishment of his kingdom.

Jesus is the King of the kingdom of God. We reign with him and submit to his authority. (Revelation 5:10, 11:15-17) A Christian is a Christ follower.

Living for God's Purposes

We have been bought at a price, the precious blood of Jesus. We have an obligation, not to live for our sinful nature, not to live for our own purposes, but to live for God as he directs by his indwelling Spirit. (Romans 8:12, 2 Corinthians 5:15) If we have faith in Jesus, we will do what Jesus did in order to bring glory to our heavenly Father.

> I tell you the truth, anyone who has faith in me **will do what I have been doing**. He will do even greater things than these, because I am going to the Father. And **I will do whatever you ask in my name, so that the Son may bring glory to the Father**. You may ask me for anything in my name, and I will do it. John 14:12-14 (NIV)

Created to Glorify God

To love God is to live so that his glory is revealed. Glory is the radiance of God. It is as though God created us as agents to reflect his bright glory out into the universe for all to see—to see him. It was God's purpose to send Jesus as his radiant light into a dark world.

> In these last days, He has spoken to us by |His| Son. God has appointed Him heir of all things and made the universe through Him. **The Son is the radiance of God's glory and the exact expression of His nature, sustaining all things by His powerful word.** After making purification for sins, He sat down at the right hand of the Majesty on high. Hebrews 1:2-3 (HCSB)

God's purpose was not to stop with Jesus. His purpose was to multiply the radiance of his glory through many. Jesus came as one man, but now, through Jesus, we have become the radiant temple of God that expands the earth. Several times in Scripture we read about the glory of God filling the Temple. (1 Kings 8:11, 2 Chronicles 5:14, 7:1-2, Ezekeil 10:4, 43:5, Revelation 15:8) Well, we are his temple. (1 Corinthians 3:16-17, 6:19) And his will is for us to be filled with his glory and to radiate his glory out into the world.

We are to live in such a way that the dark world will see the wonderful light of Jesus Christ in and through us. Through Christ he has given each one of us his Spirit to live in and among us. The Spirit is the powerful light of God that shines as a beacon of light from each one of us. We fulfill God's purposes on earth when we shine forth his glory. We shine forth God's glory when we live according to his will and his purposes. We are to shine forth God's glory like "stars in the universe" as we live in a dark and depraved world. Our lives are to be filled with the works of God. This is his "good purpose" for us. To live for God in this way is to love God. It's not being legalistic; it is love for God, for all that he is; for he is all truth and life and the eternal way of life.

Therefore, my dear friends, as you have always obeyed—not only in my presence, but now much more in my absence—continue to work out your salvation with fear and trembling, for it is **God who works in you to will and to act according to his good purpose.**

Do everything without complaining or arguing, so that you may become blameless and pure, children of God without fault in a crooked and depraved generation, in which you **shine like stars** in the universe as you hold out the word of life—in order that I may boast on the day of Christ that I did not run or labor for nothing. Philippians 2:12-16 (NIV)

Jesus came as a light into this dark world. (John 8:12, 9:5, 12:46, 1:9) After Jesus' resurrection and return to the Father, he sent back his Spirit to live within us as his light, not just in one man, but now in millions of us as we walk this earth. Jesus has called us to be the light of the entire world.

"**You are the light of the world**. A city set on a hill cannot be hidden. Nor do people light a lamp and put it under a basket, but on a stand, and it gives light to all in the house. In the same way, **let your light**

shine before others, so that they may see your good works and give glory to your Father who is in heaven. Matthew 5:14-16 (ESV)

This is a basic understanding of the gospel, that Christ was coming into the world to save it from darkness. We have been given his light, and now we shine forth his light into a dark world. Jesus is the light. He came into the world as one man, but now he lives through his church, his body—the temple of the living God. He shines his light through us as we live according to God's purposes and will. We glorify God as we shine forth the good deeds of his Spirit.

Keep your conduct among the Gentiles honorable, so that when they speak against you as evildoers, they may **see your good deeds and glorify God** on the day of visitation. 1 Peter 2:12 (ESV)

We love God—we glorify God—when we refrain from living for the purposes of the world and sinful man and, instead, live for the glorious purposes of God as we become holy instruments for his good works as he chooses to use us.

In a large house there are articles not only of gold and silver, but also of wood and clay; **some are for noble purposes and some for ignoble**. If a man cleanses himself from the latter, he will be **an instrument for noble purposes, made holy, useful to the Master and prepared to do any good work**. 2 Timothy 2:20-21 (NIV)

Having Good Works Is Not Legalism

Some might argue that this is legalistic, that we are not saved by good works. And I would agree; we are not saved by good works, but we are saved for good works. This was God's pleasure, to have a living relationship with us. *If all we consider is what the law requires or does not require because of the death of Jesus, we have missed salvation completely.* We

157

were saved in order to become children of God. We were saved to have his life by having the nature and character of Christ living in and through us by his word and Spirit. We were saved so that we would be the righteousness of God in all of his holiness and glory. And we are not inanimate objects in his hand that are thrown aside and forgotten after their use. We are the bride of Christ who has been cleansed and made beautiful by the hand of God. We were saved in order to have a living and everlasting relationship with God in all holiness, righteousness and glory. A bride is cherished for her beauty. She is bright and clean and beautiful. We are the bride of Christ, and he has cleansed us and clothed us with his radiant adornments.

> Husbands, love your wives just as Christ loved the church and **gave himself for her to sanctify her by cleansing her with the washing of the water by the word, so that he may present the church to himself as glorious—not having a stain or wrinkle, or any such blemish, but holy and blameless**. Ephesians 5:25-27 (NET)

> Let us be glad, rejoice, and **give Him glory**, because the marriage of the Lamb has come, and **His wife has prepared herself. She was given fine linen to wear, bright and pure. For the fine linen represents the righteous acts of the saints.** Revelation 19:7-8 (HCSB)

Notice that the clothing given her to wear is not her physical beauty, but her inward beauty that radiates out through the "righteous acts" of a sanctified life. This is the powerful work of God's grace in us. Jesus gave his life for us to redeem us from our wicked life of sin and to purify us as his own people who are eager to live as Jesus lived, doing "what is good".

> For the grace of God that brings salvation has appeared to all men. It teaches us to say "No" to ungodliness and worldly passions, and to live self-controlled, upright and godly lives in this present age, while we wait for the blessed hope—the glorious appearing of our great God and Savior, Jesus Christ, who gave himself for us **to redeem us from all**

wickedness and to purify for himself a people that are his very own, eager to do what is good. Titus 2:11-14 (NIV)

Jesus gave up his life so that we would be cleansed from our old self and become empowered to put on the new self, "created to be like God in true righteousness and holiness".

You were taught, with regard to your former way of life, to **put off your old self, which is being corrupted by its deceitful desires; to be made new in the attitude of your minds; and to put on the new self, created to be like God in true righteousness and holiness.** Ephesians 4:22-24 (NIV)

Do not lie to each other, **since you have taken off your old self with its practices and have put on the new self, which is being renewed in knowledge in the image of its Creator.** Colossians 3:9-10 (NIV)

Salvation is all about having a beautiful living and intimate relationship with God. It is like being Jesus' dance partner. He is the groom and we are the bride. The guests look on as their tender hearts witness the love of a strong and handsome husband for his gloriously beautiful bride. They witness how she looks up to him with love in her eyes as he caresses her in his mighty but gentle embrace. They glide around the dance floor together as though they were one. If we look close, we will witness that her husband is leading every step, and she is willingly following his lead. And together they are oh so beautiful.

We are that bride! We can be the one on the dance floor with Jesus. All we have to do is allow him to cleanse us. He will provide the wedding garments, "bright and clean". All we have to do is to put them on. Then we can enjoy his wonderful embrace as we follow his lead through every step of life as we live our lives together with him. This is our love relationship with God. It is so glorious! And this is his purpose. It has always been his purpose, to "work out everything in conformity with the purpose of his will". And his will is that we would become the bride of Christ to the "praise of his glory".

> And he made known to us the mystery of **his will according to his good pleasure, which he purposed in Christ**, to be put into effect when the times will have reached their fulfillment—to bring all things in heaven and on earth together under one head, even Christ.
>
> In him we were also chosen, having been predestined **according to the plan of him who works out everything in conformity with the purpose of his will**, in order that we, who were the first to hope in Christ, might be for **the praise of his glory**. Ephesians 1:9-12 (NIV)

So, we can see that living for God according to his will and purpose is not legalistically working in order to gain God's acceptance of us. Rather, it is a living relationship with God that is filled with life and beauty and the glory of God. In this world—this present life—most people want to get married, and most do marry. God created marriage. He created it so that we would come to know, or at least have a glimpse of our eternal marriage with Jesus. Earthly marriages are temporary, but our marriage with God is eternal. As we long to be married, so Jesus longs to be married. He longs to be united with his bride, the bride of Christ. And we are that bride. To love God is to long for our marriage with him. It is God's purpose to provide a bride for his Son. What a glorious purpose.

The devil does not want to see this marriage happen. He is doing everything in his power to corrupt and distract and distort his bride. But he will not succeed. We look around the world today, and darkness seems to prevail. Evil seems to be making much greater advances. The devil almost seems to have stolen Jesus' bride. But the Father will not fail to provide a radiant bride for his Son.

> The LORD foils the plans of the nations; he thwarts the purposes of the peoples. But the plans of the LORD stand firm forever, the purposes of his heart through all generations. Psalm 33:10-11 (NIV)

Love for God Strives to Fulfill God's Purposes

As Christians, as a people who love God, we long for God's purposes to be fulfilled. We long for the day of Jesus' return when he will make a great separation between those who love him and those who do not. (Matthew 25:31-46) But even before his return, we strive for his will and purposes to be fulfilled each day. If we love God, we also love his purposes. And if we love his purposes, we will strive to do his will. We will even cry out to him for his will to be accomplished.

I cry out to God Most High, to God who fulfills his purpose for me. Psalm 57:2 (ESV)

The LORD will fulfill his purpose for me; your steadfast love, O LORD, endures forever. Do not forsake the work of your hands. Psalm 138:8 (ESV)

Man tends to make his own plans based on his own purposes. He works with his own intellect and his own strength. But he deceives himself if he thinks that he can fulfill his own plans if they are not in concert with God's plans and purposes. Just as the man who says there is no God is a fool, so too is the man who believes he can outmaneuver God. (Psalm 14:1, 53:1, 92:6-7, 107:17, Proverbs 28:26) We can make all of the plans we want, but in the end, God will prevail with his purposes by his will.

Many are the plans in a man's heart, but it is the LORD's purpose that prevails. Proverbs 19:21 (NIV)

A wise man loves God, because in so doing, he relies on the wisdom and purposes of God, rather than his own intellect and abilities. Those who love God have the confidence that the Almighty, whom they love, will work all things out for their good according to God's purposes. And to love God is

161

to live life in pursuit of God's purposes for their life. This is our living relationship with God, to live in accordance with his will and purposes. This is the picture of one who loves God, the one who seeks out God's will and purposes for his own life as though he does not live for himself, but for God.

> And we know that **for those who love God** all things work together for good, for those who are **called according to his purpose.** Romans 8:28 (ESV)

> So we have not stopped praying for you since we first heard about you. We ask God to give you complete knowledge of his will and to give you spiritual wisdom and understanding. **Then the way you live will always honor and please the Lord, and your lives will produce every kind of good fruit.** All the while, **you will grow as you learn to know God better and better.** Colossians 1:9-10 (NLT)

Reflection Questions

Why did God create you? How do your purposes align with his purposes? Be specific; what are you actually doing?

How do you reflect God's glory through your life? How does the world see God in how you live, your character, what you say or don't say? God is love. How does the world see God's love in your love for others?

We all have an old life. With Christ, we all have a new life (if we are truly Christians). Describe your old versus your new. Be specific about how you used to act and how you act today. Give examples of your acts, attitudes and thinking from your old life and your life today.

How do you seek to know God's purposes so that you can walk in them? How do you love God by seeking his will and purposes for the purpose of living for him?

Chapter 12

Seeking the Kingdom of God and His Righteousness

Jesus taught us to pray, "Your kingdom come. Your will be done on earth as it is in heaven." (Matthew 6:10) Jesus instructed us to seek his kingdom as a first priority in our lives. (Matthew 6:33) Jesus frequently spoke about his kingdom. He even stated that that is why he was sent, to tell about the good news of his kingdom. (Luke 4:43) After Jesus rose from the dead, he spent forty days on earth before being taken up to heaven. He spent this time speaking about his kingdom. (Acts 1:3) Jesus gave several parables to give us insight into his kingdom. (Matthew, chapters 13, 20 & 25)

Once Jesus made a very strong statement about those who would enter his kingdom. He said that the only ones to enter in would be those who did the will of his Father.

> Not everyone who says to me, 'Lord, Lord,' will enter the kingdom of heaven, but only he who does the will of my Father who is in heaven. Matthew 7:21 (NIV)

If we are saved by faith, not by works, how could Jesus make such a commanding statement? It comes back down to understanding the nature of salvation. Or in this discussion, it comes down to understanding the nature of his kingdom. It is a kingdom of love. God is love. God's will is that we love one another. Without love, his kingdom is without an eternal foundation. Love is the royal law of the kingdom of God. It is the only one needed. All other requirements are fulfilled if this one is obeyed.

If you really keep the **royal law** found in Scripture, **"Love your neighbor as yourself,"** you are doing right. James 2:8 (NIV)

Those who love God—those who obey his command to love one another—will inherit his kingdom.

Listen, my dear brothers: Has not God chosen those who are poor in the eyes of the world to be rich in faith and to **inherit the kingdom he promised those who love him**? James 2:5 (NIV)

When Jesus comes to complete the establishment of his kingdom, he is going to separate the people into those who will inherit his kingdom and those who will not. And how will he separate them into two groups? He will assess how they loved one another. This is not a parable with hidden meanings. Jesus is speaking very directly about those who will inherit his kingdom and those who will not. It should also be understood from his words that to inherit his kingdom is to enter into eternal life. And those who are denied his kingdom are those who will receive eternal punishment in the eternal fire along with the devil and his rebellious angels.

"When the Son of Man comes in his glory and all the angels with him, then he will sit on his glorious throne. All the nations will be assembled before him, and he will separate people one from another like a shepherd separates the sheep from the goats. He will put the sheep on his right and the goats on his left. Then the king will say to those on his right, 'Come, you who are blessed by my Father, **inherit the kingdom prepared for you from the foundation of the world**. For I was hungry and you gave me food, I was thirsty and you gave me something to drink, I was a stranger and you invited me in, I was naked and you gave me clothing, I was sick and you took care of me, I was in prison and you visited me.' Then the righteous will answer him, 'Lord, when did we see you hungry and feed you, or thirsty and give you something to drink? When did we see you a stranger and invite you in, or naked and clothe you? When did we see you sick or in prison and visit you?' And the king will answer them, **'I tell you the truth, just as you did it for one of the least of these brothers or sisters of mine, you did it for me.'**

"Then he will say to those on his left, 'Depart from me, you accursed, into the eternal fire that has been prepared for the devil and his angels! For I was hungry and you gave me nothing to eat, I was thirsty and you gave me nothing to drink. I was a stranger and you did not receive me as a guest, naked and you did not clothe me, sick and in prison and you did not visit me.' Then they too will answer, 'Lord, when did we see you hungry or thirsty or a stranger or naked or sick or in prison, and did not give you whatever you needed?' Then he will answer them, **'I tell you the truth, just as you did not do it for one of the least of these, you did not do it for me.' And these will depart into eternal punishment, but the righteous into eternal life."** Matthew 25:31-46 (NET)

How do we love Jesus? According to his words, we love Jesus by loving one another. How does that happen? Does Jesus consider it love because we did what he commanded? That is part of it. We love God by obeying him. But there is much more here than doing what he commanded. We are the body of Christ. Jesus lives within every born again Christian by his Spirit. When we love another Christian, we directly love Jesus. This may be a mystery, but true just the same. Jesus is the brother in Christ in prison that you visited. Jesus is the brother who is hungry and you fed him. Jesus is the stranger you invited in. Jesus is the poor man you clothed. Jesus is the sick person you cared for.

And it goes a step further. Jesus lives within me. When I love someone else, I am being Jesus to them. I love them with the love of Jesus.

What a beautiful kingdom God is establishing. This kingdom is our eternal hope. To seek his kingdom, we must walk in love, for his kingdom is founded on love. We naturally strive for what we desire. Those who are not striving for the kingdom of God do not desire it. God is love. We have to love to be in his presence. Why would anyone think that in the end that they would somehow escape being cast from the presence of God when they did not seek his presence in this life? Some may plead ignorance. That is why Jesus came, to bring the truth about his kingdom, a kingdom that is founded on love. Now that we know, how can we disobey his command to love?

Love Is Not Easy

It is not always easy to love. To love we have to give up of our selves. We have internal opposition to love, for our sinful nature strives to look out for our own welfare above the welfare of others. But Jesus came and lived in a body just like ours. He was born in poverty. He was God, yet came as a man. He had nothing that set him above other men in regard to worldly possessions or status. He knew firsthand what it meant to love sacrificially—to the point of giving up his own life. So we have no excuse. We cannot plead that God does not know what it is like living on earth among other sinners. Instead, we are instructed to have the same humble attitude as that of Jesus Christ. (Philippians 2:1-8) He is our model.

Jesus said that if those of the world persecuted him, they will persecute us also. And we are to love them and pray for them. God is love, and we are to strive to be perfect in love as our heavenly Father is perfect love. In doing so, we are "sons of our Father who is in heaven".

> "You have heard that it was said, 'You shall love your neighbor and hate your enemy.' But I say to you, Love your enemies and pray for those who persecute you, **so that you may be sons of your Father who is in heaven**. For he makes his sun rise on the evil and on the good, and sends rain on the just and on the unjust. For if you love those who love

you, what reward do you have? Do not even the tax collectors do the same? And if you greet only your brothers, what more are you doing than others? Do not even the Gentiles do the same? **You therefore must be perfect, as your heavenly Father is perfect.** Matthew 5:43-48 (ESV)

Those who seek the kingdom of God—the kingdom of love—will love no matter what the cost. It means that we love even our enemies. It means that we will love even when subjected to persecution, and we do so for the sake of the kingdom.

"Blessed are those who are persecuted for righteousness, **for the kingdom of heaven belongs to them.**

"Blessed are you when people insult you and persecute you and say all kinds of evil things about you falsely on account of me. Rejoice and be glad because your reward is great in heaven, for they persecuted the prophets before you in the same way. Matthew 5:10-12 (NET)

Jesus will return to fully establish his kingdom, separate from the kingdom of this world we now live. And when he returns with his kingdom, love in the kingdom of God will not be burdensome because everyone there will walk in love. We won't have any enemies in the kingdom of God. But for now, we live in this world, and we do have enemies who will persecute us and sin against us. But we are children of the kingdom, and we are to live like we are its citizens now. We will be required to love our enemies for Jesus' sake. We will be subject to persecution for Jesus' sake— for the love of Jesus and his kingdom. This is love for God and his kingdom. In terms of persecution and our love for our enemies, we are no different than Jesus in this world. As subjects of his kingdom, we are to live as Jesus our King lived as he walked this earth and was subject to the evil of the world. To love Jesus is to live for him, which may mean that we die for him. (John 15:18-21)

Is this kind of love difficult—that is, suffering hardships and even being persecuted for Christ? Absolutely! Is it impossible for us who have heard the truth and have been called out of the kingdom of this world and into the kingdom of God? Absolutely not! Those of us who have heard, who are chosen and have received his Spirit are without excuse. Look at Jesus' words above again. We will be persecuted. This is Jesus talking! Do you believe him? He meant exactly what he said. If we love Jesus, we will do what he says.

"Why do you call me, 'Lord, Lord,' and do not do what I say? Luke 6:46 (NIV)

One day Jesus told his disciples the kind of suffering that he was about to endure on the cross. Then he told them that they needed to deny themselves and take up their cross. In other words, they were to subject themselves to the sins of others without retaliation, out of love for Jesus and love for their enemies. And he said that this was a requirement for being one of his followers. Do we believe Jesus? If so, do we live out his truth? Do we deny ourselves for Jesus' sake? Do we lose our lives for his sake? Do we truly love him?

And he said to all, "If anyone would come after me, let him deny himself and take up his cross daily and follow me. For whoever would save his life will lose it, but whoever loses his life for my sake will save it. For what does it profit a man if he gains the whole world and loses or forfeits himself? For whoever is ashamed of me and of my words, of him will the Son of Man be ashamed when he comes in his glory and the glory of the Father and of the holy angels. Luke 9:23-26 (ESV)

God is not fooled by our duplicity and false confessions. We serve and live for what we love. Just as Jesus said that we cannot serve both God and money, for we will love one and hate the other (Matthew 6:24), the same can be said for the kingdom of God and the kingdom of this world. We will choose to serve the one we love most. Which one do we treasure? That is the one we will serve and love.

> For where your treasure is, there your heart will be also. Matthew 6:21 (ESV)

Reflection Questions

Why is it impossible to seek the kingdom of God without loving others?

Jesus instructed us to pray for his kingdom to come and his will to be done on earth. He also told us to seek his kingdom as a first priority. What does that look like in your life? What do you decisively do to make this happen? Remember what you just concluded about love.

Peter instructed us, "Always be prepared to give an answer to everyone who asks you to give the reason for the hope that you have". 1 Peter 3:15 (NIV) Describe your hope in the kingdom of God. Describe this wonderful kingdom and how it functions.

Chapter 13

Enduring Persecution
Is Love for God

What is persecution? In a statement, persecution is the giving up of anything in our lives, including life itself, in the face of opposition from others for the sake of living for Jesus Christ in whatever manner he calls us to. Persecution is not an excuse for our being rebellious, although we still have to live by our conscience and do what is right in the eyes of God in spite of the consequences. Persecution is standing up for God in the face of opposition. It is never done with the intent of causing conflict. Persecution comes from the anger of those who oppose the truth about God and all that exists, even though we come in peace and love and truth. They persecute those who proclaim the truth in order to suppress the truth.

> For the wrath of God is revealed from heaven against all ungodliness and unrighteousness of men, **who by their unrighteousness suppress the truth**. Romans 1:18 (ESV)

Persecution comes in many forms. For example, a Christian son or daughter of a non-Christian family may be rejected by the rest of the family for what they believe and how they express their faith. The rejection may be just ridicule, but it may become much more severe if the rest of the family adheres to another set of beliefs that opposes Christianity, such as

Islam. They could be thrown out of the family such that all contact is forbidden.

Persecution can come from the government, who may suppress the truth through laws that prohibit certain types of speech in certain environments. An example may be prohibiting pastors from taking political stands with their congregation. We have "hate crimes" now for Christians who oppose homosexuality. Not only are we being told we cannot speak out against such behavior, we are told that we must support it. If you have a wedding cake business, you cannot deny making one for a same-sex wedding. If you take wedding pictures for a living, you cannot refuse to do a same-sex wedding. Freedom of speech and religion may be part of the Constitution, but we are seeing these rights heavily challenged for Christians who choose to live their faith in their daily lives.

Persecution has no limits. Many around the world are tortured, imprisoned and murdered for promoting their Christian faith. This has not happened yet in the United States, but it may soon come. ISIS has ruthlessly taken the lives of many Christians in the East. And we have seen the murder of many Americans and Europeans by ideological Islamic terrorists.

Christian persecution, including imprisonment, harsh treatment and even death is not limited to countries where Islam dominates the land. Communist nations have been persecuting Christians for decades, and still do today. For example persecution is very prevalent in China and North Korea. Ultimately, persecution is the devil's work, and he uses governments and non-Christian religions to harshly and even violently oppose Christians.

More people are martyred around the world today than ever before. Numbers vary because of the difficulty of tracking such deaths, but the estimates range from over 100,000 to over 170,000 every year. David B. Barrett, Todd M. Johnson, and Peter F. Crossing reported in the International Bulletin of Missionary Research (Vol. 33, No. 1: 32) that 176,000 were martyred for their Christian faith in mid-2008 to mid-2009. The Voice of the Martyrs, who support the martyrs around the world, made these comments:

It is impossible to know with absolute certainty the exact number of Christians killed for their faith each year. However, according to the World Evangelical Alliance, more than 200 million Christians in at least 60 countries are denied fundamental human rights solely because of their faith.

Much of today's persecution still takes place in remote areas of countries often cut off from or with restricted access to modern communications. Most martyrs suffer and die anonymously—unknown and forgotten—their deaths unrecorded except in heaven. What is reported often occurs weeks, months and even years after the fact. Persecution is often such a part of life that it hardly dawns on the afflicted to tell the world. Even then, many are nervous about sharing what they know for fear of retribution. ("Voice of the Martyrs")[4]

In the United States we boast of religious freedom; not one person is martyred. However, by a judgment of the U.S. Supreme Court, prayer was removed from public schools in 1962. The Bible was removed in 1963. And the Ten Commandments were removed in 1980 and have been taken down in most public places. Immoral and unrighteous behavior is raised up and protected throughout our land. And Christians are persecuted for standing up for their religious convictions. Clearly, a battle rages in the United States over who is Lord: Jesus or Satan.

It should be obvious that enduring persecution in its various forms is a deliberate act of loving God with all of our strength. To love God is to stand up for God in the face of those who hate him.

---

4 . "FAQ: How many Christians are killed for their faith every year?." *The Voice of the Martyrs.* The Voice of the Martyrs, n.d. Web. 20 Sep 2012. <http://www.persecution.net/faq.htm>.

Jesus Was Persecuted

Jesus came with the purpose of bringing life to mankind by bringing his truth to us—by leading us to turn from our destructive way of life and to live in a new way that brings eternal life (repentance). (John 14:6) He came to bring forgiveness of our sins so that our relationship with God would be reconciled. He came, was killed and rose from the dead in order to send his Spirit to live within us, to give us new hearts and to empower us to live with God's character from our hearts.

This all sounds so wonderful! Who would want to oppose Jesus? But when he walked upon this earth, he was opposed, rejected, slandered, falsely accused, tortured and killed. Persecution is the rejection of Jesus. *The hateful rejection of Jesus is the definition of persecution. Man rejected Jesus when he walked this earth, but now we are the body of Jesus walking this earth. Jesus was persecuted to the point of his death, and now those of the world persecute Jesus by their attacks upon all who proclaim to bear his name and profess Jesus in their lives.* Jesus was very clear that if they persecuted him, we, too, would be persecuted.

If the world hates you, be aware that it hated me first. If you belonged to the world, the world would love you as its own. However, because you do not belong to the world, but I chose you out of the world, for this reason the world hates you. Remember what I told you, 'A slave is not greater than his master.' **If they persecuted me, they will also persecute you.** If they obeyed my word, they will obey yours too. But **they will do all these things to you on account of my name,** because they do not know the one who sent me. If I had not come and spoken to them, they would not be guilty of sin. But they no longer have any excuse for their sin. **The one who hates me hates my Father too.** If I had not performed among them the miraculous deeds that no one else did, they would not be guilty of sin. But now they have seen the deeds and have **hated both me and my Father.** Now this happened to fulfill the word that is written in their law, '**They hated me without reason**.' John 15:18-25 (NET)

In Matthew 24 Jesus tells about the signs of the end of time. He describes how sin, the works of the devil, war and evil will increase. The end is the culmination of hatred for Jesus. False prophets and messiahs will arise and Jesus will be opposed by the world at every level. Jesus said that in this time the persecution of Jesus will intensify for those who profess his name.

Then you will be handed over to be persecuted and put to death, and **you will be hated by all nations because of me**. Matthew 24:9 (NIV)

There is a clear division among mankind between those who hate him and those who love him. *If we love Jesus, we will be hated by the world that rejects Jesus.* We must ask ourselves these questions: Do we love Jesus? Do we side with the world when in the world? Do we hide Jesus so that we are not rejected? To love Jesus is to take a firm side with him. We either acknowledge him among those who would reject him or we hide him. The consequences are severe. Our behavior is witness to our love for him.

So everyone who acknowledges me before men, I also will acknowledge before my Father who is in heaven, but whoever denies me before men, I also will deny before my Father who is in heaven.
"Do not think that I have come to bring peace to the earth. I have not come to bring peace, but a sword. For I have come to set a man against his father, and a daughter against her mother, and a daughter-in-law against her mother-in-law. And a person's enemies will be those of his own household. **Whoever loves father or mother more than me is not worthy of me, and whoever loves son or daughter more than me is not worthy of me.** And whoever does not take his cross and follow me is not worthy of me. Whoever finds his life will lose it, and whoever loses his life for my sake will find it. Matthew 10:32-39 (ESV)

This is not a random, unexplained persecution. Jesus sends us out to proclaim him to a lost and dark world, and in so doing, we come under persecution. We have been sent, and persecution will come. Will we go? Will we chose to love Jesus? (Matthew 10:16-39)

To love God is to be willing to risk our lives in the face of others who will reject or even hate us for our identity with Jesus. It may cost us our relationships. It may affect our livelihood. It may affect our freedom. It may bring about severe suffering. Jesus gave up his life and was persecuted on a cross. Are we willing to give up our lives for Jesus? Are we willing to take up our cross for Jesus' namesake?

A Battle Between Kingdoms

Jesus taught us to pray, "Your kingdom come. Your will be done on earth as it is in heaven." He taught us to seek his kingdom and his righteousness as a first priority of our lives. And he said that his kingdom was not of this world.

> Jesus replied, "**My kingdom is not from this world**. If my kingdom were from this world, my servants would be fighting to keep me from being handed over to the Jewish authorities. But as it is, my kingdom is not from here." John 18:36 (NET)

There is an intense battle on this earth. It is a battle between the kingdom of this world and the kingdom of God. Everyone has taken a side. Either they are living for the prosperity of the kingdom of God or for the prosperity of the kingdom of this world. Either we stand up for the kingdom of this world or we stand up for the kingdom of God.

> You adulterous people, **don't you know that friendship with the world is hatred toward God? Anyone who chooses to be a friend of the world becomes an enemy of God**. James 4:4 (NIV)

Those who fight for the world hate those who are of the kingdom of God. There is no peace between the two kingdoms. Jesus came to bring the victory of his kingdom, and his kingdom is a kingdom of peace within. But there will be no peace between his kingdom and the world. In fact, Jesus came to bring about a clear division between the two.

Do you think I have come to bring peace on earth? No, I tell you, but rather division! Luke 12:51 (NET)

Those of the world persecuted Jesus, and they will persecute those who are truly of him. When we take a stand for Jesus' kingdom, we expose ourselves to persecution by the world. If we love Jesus, we will be hated by the world. (John 15:18-21)

This is love for God, to live for God as opposed to living for the world. The battle is twofold for us. First, we have to abstain from the ways of the world in order to live for the ways of God's kingdom. And secondly, when we take a stand for God's kingdom, we have set ourselves up for rejection, being hated and persecuted by those of the world. This is true no matter where we live. The persecution may come in varying degrees, but it will come. Persecution may be as light as a disgusting look and as severe as torture, imprisonment and death. To love God is to overcome the world. And we overcome the world by remaining separate from the world and by enduring the persecution that will come.

Everyone who believes that Jesus is the Christ has been born of God, and everyone who loves the Father loves whoever has been born of him. By this we know that we love the children of God, when we love God and obey his commandments. For **this is the love of God, that we keep his commandments**. And his commandments are not burdensome. For **everyone who has been born of God overcomes the world. And this is the victory that has overcome the world—our faith.**

177

Who is it that overcomes the world except the one who believes that Jesus is the Son of God? 1 John 5:1-5 (ESV)

Richard Wurmbrand was a pastor in communist Romania in the late 1940's. One day Richard and his wife Sabina were at a conference of pastors and members of the communist party. Many pastors were being coerced into proclaiming that Christianity and communism could coexist. Richard disagreed, but for the moment remained silent for fear of what the communists would do to him if he opposed them. But Sabina challenged him. Richard recollects the conversation:

> Sabina told me, "Richard, stand up and wash away this shame from the face of Christ! They are spitting in His face." I said to her, "If I do so, you lose your husband." She replied, "I don't wish to have a coward as a husband."[5]

So Wurmbrand stood up in protest. He was soon imprisoned for his outward vocal stand against anti-Christian communism. He was tortured, brainwashed and starved. He spent three years in solitary confinement with no sound and no light. After eight and a half years of imprisonment, he was released and was warned not to preach again. But Pastor Wurmbrand continued to preach and teach in the underground church. Three years after his release he was abducted again and sent back to prison for five more years.

God used Wurmbrand's fourteen years of persecution to motivate him to spend the rest of his life informing and leading others in support of persecuted Christians around the world. After his release he started Voice of the Martyrs, a mission to raise awareness of and support to the many

---

[5] Wurmbrand, Richard. *Tortured for Christ*. Bartlesville, OK: Living Sacrifice Book, 1998. Print.

thousands of persecuted Christians who are imprisoned, tortured and even martyred for their open beliefs.[6]

This is just one story of a persecuted Christian. There are many more that have gone unnoticed. I recommend reading *The Heavenly Man*, by Yun. This is an autobiographical account of a man who was instrumental in the founding of the persecuted Christian house churches of China. He tells of the imprisonment and torture that he received as a consequence of living out his faith in a nation that persecutes Christians. He also tells of how God miraculously used him, healed him and opened the gates of prison.

Thousands around the world have been severely persecuted and are willing to die for Christ. Persecution is coming to the United States. Are we willing to die for Christ? Are we even willing to live for him? Do we love him enough?

There is an intense battle between these two kingdoms, the kingdom of this dark world and the kingdom of God. Persecution is present, and it is intensifying. There was a day when being a Christian was generally considered a good thing in America. In public today, we are looked down upon, if not forbidden, to even mention Jesus, God or what the Bible says about anything. Most workplaces compel us to keep our faith private so as not to take sides or offend anyone. But when Jesus returns, the battle will be over, and victory will be proclaimed. The dark kingdom of this world will be fully exposed and destroyed. It will be plundered and handed over to Christ. Jesus' kingdom will reign forever, and we will reign with him.

> Then the seventh angel blew his trumpet, and there were loud voices in heaven saying: **"The kingdom of the world has become the kingdom of our Lord and of his Christ, and he will reign for ever and ever."** Revelation 11:15 (NET)

---

[6] www.persecution.com This is the Voice of the Martyrs website. Learn how you can become informed and involved.

They were singing a new song: "You are worthy to take the scroll and to open its seals because you were killed, and at the cost of your own blood **you have purchased for God persons from every tribe, language, people, and nation. You have appointed them as a kingdom and priests to serve our God, and they will reign on the earth**." Revelation 5:9-10 (NET)

When this occurs, we will understand how those who are persecuted for Christ's sake are the ones who are blessed.

"Blessed are those who are persecuted for righteousness' sake, for theirs is the kingdom of heaven.

"Blessed are you when others revile you and persecute you and utter all kinds of evil against you falsely on my account. Rejoice and be glad, for your reward is great in heaven, for so they persecuted the prophets who were before you. Matthew 5:10-12 (ESV)

We see the blessing when we see the final outcome. The wicked may appear intimidating and in control today, but their power will come to an end, and then it will be their turn to be tormented. There are no good blessings apart from God. In the end, we will be perfectly united with God, but those who deny Christ and persecute those who profess his name will be cast out of his presence forever. This was the contemplation of the psalmist when he saw the prosperity of the wicked, but then he understood their final outcome.

Then I entered the precincts of God's temple, and understood the destiny of the wicked. Psalm 73:17 (NET)

Loving God and loving Jesus today is lived out in this evil world through faith that we have in the eternal future with God in his kingdom to come.

Reflection Questions

Do you see the battle between kingdoms here on earth? Describe what you have seen.

How might you become engaged in the battles?

Do you stand up for Jesus among others? How do you testify to Jesus among your family members? Among your work associates? With your neighbors? In society in what you stand for and what you will not succumb to?

Do you pray in public? Do you publically pray before you eat at a restaurant? When alone in a public place? When with your family? When with work associates or friends?

Chapter 14

Maintaining Our Love for God

So now that we have studied our love for God, is it just a matter of filling our lives with a long list of do's and don'ts? If I diligently read God's word, if I pray, if I seek to align my purposes with God's, if I exercise faith in all things, if I decisively love others, if I seek to understand and live for God's kingdom and if I acknowledge Jesus in all places to all people, subjecting myself to persecution, even death—then, have I loved God with all my heart, soul, mind and strength? Is there something more?

Love Is Not a Set of Rules

This study began with a teacher of the law asking Jesus which command was the greatest. Remember, it was the teachers of the law and other high level officials of the church at the time that rejected Jesus and had him crucified. These men thought that they loved God. They raised up the written word and the law. They practiced all of the ordnances proscribed by God. They met in the temple daily. Did they not love God? It does not take much reading or insight to realize that they did not love God. So what is the difference between someone who does and someone who does not?

King Saul—Humility to Pride

What about Saul, Israel's first king. He was chosen by God from all of the tribes of Israel. He was handpicked and anointed by God as king.

> Then Samuel took a small container of olive oil and poured it on Saul's head. Samuel kissed him and said, **"The LORD has chosen you to lead his people Israel!** You will rule over the LORD's people and you will deliver them from the power of the enemies who surround them. This will be your sign that **the LORD has chosen you as leader over his inheritance**. 1 Samuel 10:1 (NET)

Not only was Saul handpicked by God to be king over Israel, God also made him into a different person and gave Saul a new heart so that he could perform the task of leading God's nation.

> The Spirit of the LORD will come upon you in power, and you will prophesy with them; and **you will be changed into a different person**. Once these signs are fulfilled, do whatever your hand finds to do, for God is with you. 1 Samuel 10:6-7 (NIV)

> As Saul turned to leave Samuel, **God changed Saul's heart**, and all these signs were fulfilled that day. When they arrived at Gibeah, a procession of prophets met him; the Spirit of God came upon him in power, and he joined in their prophesying. 1 Samuel 10:9-10 (NIV)

God anointed Saul with his Spirit. Saul even prophesied by God's Spirit. He was given great authority and power to rise up against Israel's enemy nations, and he had many victories. But before his calling and anointing, Saul was humble. He didn't think he was qualified because he came from the smallest tribe of Israel, the tribe of Benjamin. (1 Samuel 9:21) When the time came to announce him as king, he hid among the supply bags. (1 Samuel 10:22)

Saul was thirty years old when he began to reign, and was king for forty-two years. As time progressed, Saul won many battles. He no longer thought of himself as a shy man from the smallest tribe. He was now a powerful king. He also began to see himself as the powerful one, and he lost sight of God's sovereignty over his life. He lost sight of the fact that God had changed and anointed him for the kingship. All of his greatness, power and victories were due to God's choosing, anointing and presence. But that recognition faded as Saul became great in his own eyes. Over these years he lost his heart for God—he became proud. This was the problem with the Pharisees and teachers of the law as well. They may have been appointed by God for the keeping and teaching of his word, they may have been appointed with authority over God's people, but their hearts were far from knowing and loving God. The position God gave them had corrupted their hearts as they became proud. They thought that everything depended upon them—their knowledge, their positions of authority, their lordship and anything that raised them up in the eyes of man.

One day, Saul and his army were hiding in fear from the Philistine army. Samuel told Saul to wait for him before moving ahead. Samuel was to sacrifice a burnt offering to the Lord before entering into battle. Samuel was the priest, and, according to God's dictates, only Samuel the priest could offer up the burnt offering. But Saul became fearful and impatient and went ahead of God and Samuel. He had trusted in his own strength and lost sight of God's power that worked in and through him.

Samuel said, "What have you done?" And Saul said, "When I saw that the people were scattering from me, and that you did not come within the days appointed, and that the Philistines had mustered at Michmash, I said, 'Now the Philistines will come down against me at Gilgal, and I have not sought the favor of the LORD.' So I forced myself, and offered the burnt offering." And Samuel said to Saul, "You have done foolishly. **You have not kept the command of the LORD your God, with which he commanded you**. For then the LORD would have established your kingdom over Israel forever. But now your kingdom shall not continue. **The LORD has sought out a man after his own heart, and the LORD has commanded him to be prince over his people, because you have not kept what the LORD commanded you."** 1 Samuel 13:11-14 (ESV)

Notice that God proclaimed that he would remove Saul as king, and give the leadership to a "man after his own heart". Saul's heart may have begun humble, but now his heart had become self-sufficiently proud.

It is all too easy to begin in the right vain with God—loving him, serving him, worshiping him and living for him. But the grace of God, the calling of God and the anointing that accompanies these callings can draw our heartfelt focus from seeing and knowing God to a focus on ourselves. We can become corrupted by our own beauty and anointing, the beauty and anointing God has bestowed upon us.

Lucifer Became the Devil—Beauty to Pride

Pride was the devil's fall. He was created with great beauty and power, but they became his downfall. Initially, the devil was created as a magnificent angel, a "guardian cherub". His name was Lucifer.[7] It was his magnificence that brought him down through pride.

> **You were the seal of perfection, full of wisdom and perfect in beauty.** You were in Eden, the garden of God. Every kind of precious stone covered you: carnelian, topaz, and diamond, beryl, onyx, and jasper, sapphire, turquoise and emerald. Your mountings and settings were crafted in gold; they were prepared on the day you were created. You **were an anointed guardian cherub,** for I had appointed you. You were on the holy mountain of God; you walked among the fiery stones. **From**

---

[7] The name Lucifer comes from the King James translation of Isaiah 14:12. The NIV translation describes him with the name "O morning star, son of the dawn". The ESV uses "O Day Star, son of Dawn". This is essentially what Lucifer means when translating the Hebrew word helel, as found in the Hebrew text.

the day you were created you were blameless in your ways until wickedness was found in you. Ezekiel 28:12-15 (HCSB)

Your heart became proud because of your beauty; For the sake of your splendor you corrupted your wisdom. So I threw you down to the earth; I made you a spectacle before kings. Ezekiel 28:17 (HCSB)

Think about it. God created this magnificent angel and endowed him with beauty and power. Then, as Lucifer considered his beauty and power that came from God, he thought that he was now capable of raising himself up above his creator. Pride blinds us and lies to us, and corrupts our hearts such that we welcome and believe the lie. Lucifer's own power and beauty, that came from God, became his source of pride, which began his downfall.

How you have fallen from heaven, O morning star, son of the dawn! You have been cast down to the earth, you who once laid low the nations! **You said in your heart, "I will ascend to heaven; I will raise my throne above the stars of God; I will sit enthroned on the mount of assembly, on the utmost heights of the sacred mountain. I will ascend above the tops of the clouds; I will make myself like the Most High."** But you are brought down to the grave, to the depths of the pit. Isaiah 14:12-15 (NIV)

Just because we may have started out with God's anointed beauty and power does not give any assurance that we will walk in love for God the rest of our lives. *We may begin loving God, but we can easily stray from love to pride.* The outward behavior may even look like love for God, but the heart may be filled with selfish pride. This was the heart of the devil. This was the heart of the Pharisees. This was the heart of Saul, even as he was still going out to battle, fighting for the kingdom of Israel. But on account of his pride, he began to take things into his own hands, doing things his own way instead of being humbly obedient to God.

186

Affirmation from Man Rather than God

Something else happens when we become proud. One would think that if we were proud, we would not care so much about what others thought of us. But that is not how we are created. We all care about what others think. We all seek to become honored by others. *If we truly love God, we seek our approval from God above the approval of men. It is his affirmation that overrides anyone else's. This is the walk of someone who loves God. The proud have replaced God's approval with the approval of men.* This is what happened to Saul. He was afraid of what his people would think of him, so he gave into their demands.

> Then Saul said to Samuel, "I have sinned. I violated the LORD's command and your instructions. **I was afraid of the people and so I gave in to them**. 1 Samuel 15:24 (NIV)

This fear of man's opinion was what Aaron faced when Moses was up on the mountain with the Lord, when the people began to lose their heart toward God because Moses was gone for so long. They became impatient and began to complain to Aaron. So Aaron collected all their gold jewelry and fashioned a golden calf for them to worship.

> And Moses said to Aaron, "What did this people do to you that you have brought such a great sin upon them?" And Aaron said, "Let not the anger of my lord burn hot. You know the people, that they are set on evil. For they said to me, 'Make us gods who shall go before us. As for this Moses, the man who brought us up out of the land of Egypt, we do not know what has become of him.' So I said to them, 'Let any who have gold take it off.' So they gave it to me, and I threw it into the fire, and out came this calf." Exodus 32:21-24 (ESV)

Aaron gave in to the pressures of the people rather than taking a stand of obedience to God. Saul fell to the same pressures. The challenge is to obey God rather than man. Aaron failed in this regard, and so did Saul. This failure to obey God rather than man began with Adam, who had to choose between his wife's command and God's. He quickly chose to do as his wife commanded. And a curse came upon Adam for obeying his wife rather than God. God had clearly spoken to him, commanding him not to eat of the tree of the knowledge of good and evil. But Adam willfully chose to obey his wife's command instead.

> And to Adam he said, "**Because you have listened to the voice of your wife and have eaten of the tree of which I commanded you, 'You shall not eat of it,'** cursed is the ground because of you; in pain you shall eat of it all the days of your life; thorns and thistles it shall bring forth for you; and you shall eat the plants of the field. Genesis 3:17-18 (ESV)

God's Anointing Can Be Removed as Easily as It Is Given

One day God commanded Saul to fight against the Amalekites and totally destroy them, not leaving anything alive or taking any plunder. That was God's command, but that is not what he did. His men wanted the plunder, so that is what they took.

> But Saul and the army spared Agag and the best of the sheep and cattle, the fat calves and lambs—everything that was good. These they were unwilling to destroy completely, but everything that was despised and weak they totally destroyed.
> Then the word of the LORD came to Samuel: **"I am grieved that I have made Saul king, because he has turned away from me and has not carried out my instructions."** Samuel was troubled, and he cried out to the LORD all that night. 1 Samuel 15:9-11 (NIV)

Saul started his reign being humble, but his prideful disobedience brought him down. The anointing that God placed on Saul was taken from him. The anointing did not actually belong to Saul. Like any anointing, it belongs to God. He can give it and he can take it back. He gives to the humble, but he brings down the prideful.

Humble yourselves before the Lord, and he will exalt you. James 4:10 (ESV)

But he gives more grace. Therefore it says, **"God opposes the proud, but gives grace to the humble."** James 4:6 (ESV)

And that is what God did to Saul. When he was humble, he raised him up as king. When he became proud, he rejected him and removed his blessing from him.

But Samuel replied, "What is more pleasing to the LORD: your burnt offerings and sacrifices or your obedience to his voice? Listen! **Obedience is better than sacrifice, and submission is better than offering the fat of rams. Rebellion is as sinful as witchcraft, and stubbornness as bad as worshiping idols. So because you have rejected the command of the LORD, he has rejected you as king**." 1 Samuel 15:22-23 (NLT)

Saul became proud, which led to rebellion, disobedience and stubbornness. This is not a heart that loves God. God is not fooled, and God can remove a blessings as quickly as he gives it. The Lord was seeking a man after his own heart. Saul was not that man, which he demonstrated through his disobedience.

But now your kingdom shall not continue. **The LORD has sought out a man after his own heart**, and the LORD has commanded him to be prince over his people, because you have not kept what the LORD commanded you." 1 Samuel 13:14 (ESV)

The proverbs of Solomon warn us several times about the downfall that awaits the proud. We would be wise to heed the warning, but, unfortunately, pride can blind us to the warning. We need to take special precautions while we are still humble.

Pride comes before destruction, and an arrogant spirit before a fall. Better to be lowly of spirit with the humble than to divide plunder with the proud. Proverbs 16:18-19 (HCSB)

When pride comes, disgrace follows, but with humility comes wisdom. Proverbs 11:2 (HCSB)

Before his downfall a man's heart is proud, but humility comes before honor. Proverbs 18:12 (HCSB)

Much of the time pride will be at the root of a downfall, but the downfall has the power to bring us to a place of humility where we may be restored.

A person's pride will humble him, but a humble spirit will gain honor. Proverbs 29:23 (HCSB)

King David—Humility to Pride

Saul was rejected because of his prideful, disobedient heart. So the Lord sought out another man for king, one who had a submissive, thankful and obedient heart toward the Lord.

After removing Saul, he made David their king. He testified concerning him: **'I have found David son of Jesse a man after my own heart; he will do everything I want him to do.'** Acts 13:22 (NIV)

David was a shepherd boy at this time. The Lord rejected Saul as king, and was about to have David anointed king. David started out humble and had a heartfelt drive to fight for God's honor. About this time, a huge giant of a man, Goliath, from the Philistine army, came against the Israeli armies. He came out daily to challenge any man who was brave enough to fight. But there was no one brave enough to accept his challenge, so he came back every day with his defiant prodding. He used boastful words and defamed God's people. One day, David happened to hear the giant's words, and he was set in his heart to be the one to fight. So he went to King Saul to ask for permission to come against him.

David said to Saul, "Let no one lose heart on account of this Philistine; your servant will go and fight him."

Saul replied, "You are not able to go out against this Philistine and fight him; **you are only a boy, and he has been a fighting man from his youth.**"

But David said to Saul, "Your servant has been keeping his father's sheep. When a lion or a bear came and carried off a sheep from the flock, I went after it, struck it and rescued the sheep from its mouth. When it turned on me, I seized it by its hair, struck it and killed it. **Your servant has killed both the lion and the bear; this uncircumcised Philistine will be like one of them, because he has defied the armies of the living God. The LORD who delivered me from the paw of the lion and the paw of the bear will deliver me from the hand of this Philistine.**"

Saul said to David, "Go, and the LORD be with you." 1 Samuel 17:32-37 (NIV)

At this point David was humble and heartfelt for God's honor and his people. He expresses his humility when he proclaimed that God is the one who gave him victory over the loin and the bear, and that his battle against the giant would be no different. Obviously, the boy David was no match for the giant Goliath, who was an experienced soldier. But David was not going in his own strength. He said that the Lord would deliver him. And David was outraged with the giant's vulgarities against God's people.

We all know the outcome. David went after the giant with a sling and a stone. He killed him and cut his head off with the giant's own sword. But now let's flash ahead several years. David had taken the throne. He had become a great warrior. He had engaged in many battles against enemy nations and had come home with the victories. Israel's army had grown, and now David had begun to think that his might and power resided in the size of his magnificent army and his own ability to lead. He began to lose sight of the truth—God was his strength, and only in God was there victory. So one day David wanted to know how large his army had become. He wanted to measure his power by knowing the number of his troops.

Satan rose up against Israel and incited David to take a census of Israel. So David said to Joab and the commanders of the troops, "Go and count the Israelites from Beersheba to Dan. Then report back to me so that I may know how many there are."

But Joab replied, "May the LORD multiply his troops a hundred times over. My lord the king, are they not all my lord's subjects? Why does my lord want to do this? Why should he bring guilt on Israel?"

The king's word, however, overruled Joab; so Joab left and went throughout Israel and then came back to Jerusalem. Joab reported the number of the fighting men to David: In all Israel there were one million one hundred thousand men who could handle a sword, including four hundred and seventy thousand in Judah.

But Joab did not include Levi and Benjamin in the numbering, because the king's command was repulsive to him. **This command was also evil in the sight of God; so he punished Israel.**

Then David said to God, "I have sinned greatly by doing this. Now, I beg you, take away the guilt of your servant. I have done a very foolish thing." 1 Chronicles 21:1-8 (NIV)

This was a very serious offense in the eyes of God. Instead of being appreciative and thankful for the power that God had endowed upon David and his kingdom, in pride, David thought that the power was due to his own abilities. As a consequence, God gave David a choice of one of three punishments.

So Gad went to David and said to him, "This is what the LORD says: 'Take your choice: three years of famine, three months of being swept away before your enemies, with their swords overtaking you, or three days of the sword of the LORD—days of plague in the land, with the angel of the LORD ravaging every part of Israel.' Now then, decide how I should answer the one who sent me." 1 Chronicles 21:11-12 (NIV)

David chose the plague. David was humbled. He confessed his sin, his pride and his disobedience. He sacrificed an offering before the Lord and pleaded with him to stop the plague, which the Lord did.

A Warning for Us

There is a strong warning for each one of us. When we first start out with the Lord, it may be natural to be humble before the Almighty God who is pouring out his power and strength through us. But, in time, it can be just as natural to become proud, thinking that we possess the power and strength apart from God's provision. We can start out with a heart for God and lose it. And this can happen without even knowing that our heart has turned from loving God to focusing on our own selfish ambitions. We all can attest to great spiritual leaders in our time who started out strong in the Lord and then fell in their prideful sin. But this warning is not just for those in high positions. It can happen to all of us. Paul refers to those who shipwrecked their faith. (1 Timothy 1:19) We need to guard our hearts at all times so as not to fall as others have.

Guard your heart above all else, for it is the source of life. Proverbs 4:23 (HCSB)

We don't have to rise to a high place of leadership in order to fall. It may be that God has delivered us from a terrible pit, such as an addiction or a serious loss, such as our job, or a crime that sent us to prison. God may have reached down to lift us out of our bondage and despair. At this point, we do not have to be in a high place to fall. We may just take for granted that we can now walk out life in our own strength. This is a perfect setup for a prideful fall.

Paul was once a Pharisee who went about persecuting Christians, even to the point of death. But one day Jesus came to him, convicted him and turned him around and used him powerfully for the establishment of Jesus' Church. Thousands of years later, we still read his letters. Jesus anointed him with his Spirit such that he had nearly all of the gifts of the Spirit. He gave him great revelations, some of which he could not describe for us and some that no one should tell. (2 Corinthians 12:1-4) Even though his past was one of persecuting Christ, now he had been given great gifts, revelations and powers that could have made him proud—that could have destroyed his relationship with and love for God. God protected him from such a calamity by keeping him weak in his flesh. We do not know his exact infirmity, but it was meant to keep him humble.

...even though I have received such wonderful revelations from God. So **to keep me from becoming proud**, I was given a thorn in my flesh, **a messenger from Satan to torment me** and **keep me from becoming proud**.

Three different times I begged the Lord to take it away. Each time he said, "My grace is all you need. **My power works best in weakness.**" So now I am glad to boast about my weaknesses, so that the power of Christ can work through me. That's why I take pleasure in my weaknesses, and in the insults, hardships, persecutions, and troubles that I suffer for Christ. For **when I am weak, then I am strong**. 2 Corinthians 12:7-10 (NLT)

When we first come to know the love of God, we may naturally respond with appreciation and even excitement. Our pursuit of him may be driven by our delightful emotions. And out of our new found life, we may do everything out of a heartfelt motivation. But the several examples given thus far should serve as a warning for all of us. We can lose what we have if we are unaware and disobedient. The loss does not come in a day or even a week. It creeps up on us. We gradually turn away from God and toward our own selfish motives and pride. We hardly notice. It is like the story of the frog in hot water. A frog is a cold blooded amphibian. His body temperature adapts to his surroundings. If you throw him into hot water, he will jump out. But if you put him in cold water and slowly heat it up, he will not notice that he is slowly being cooked to death.

It is fully possible to lose what has been given to us. Loving God with all of our heart, mind, soul and strength is a deliberate pursuit. It does not rest on our emotions. If it does, it can slowly fade and transform into rebellion or pride.

We are chosen by God. The children of Israel were chosen by God. We all need to understand that being chosen does not guarantee that we will love God in return, or that we will continue in our love for God. Look at what God said of his chosen people.

Therefore I was provoked with that generation and said, "**They always go astray in their hearts, and they have not known My ways**." Hebrews 3:10 (HCSB)

The writer of Hebrews uses their fall and their hardened hearts as a warning for all of us today. If we are not aware of the potential to fall away, we likely will—and, like the frog, we may never even notice what has happened until it is too late.

See to it, brothers, that none of you has a **sinful, unbelieving heart that turns away from the living God**. But encourage one another daily, as long as it is called Today, so that none of you may be **hardened by sin's deceitfulness**. We have come to share in Christ **if we hold firmly till the end the confidence we had at first**. As has just been said: "Today, if you hear his voice, **do not harden your hearts** as you did in the rebellion." Hebrews 3:12-15 (NIV)

What do we learn from this? It takes deliberate effort to continue to love God. We have all kinds of opposition. Our own selfishness can blind us and turn us away from God by focusing on our own agendas and cares. The world is constantly before us, tempting us and making every effort to transform our thinking. Even our so-called Christian culture can lead us astray into a pursuit of self gratification—and all in the name of Jesus.

Jesus spoke strongly to the seven churches as we read his words in the book of Revelation. His words are ones of endurance, perseverance and of a serious warning not to turn back. He admonishes us to remain steadfast and gives great eternal promises to those who "overcome". (Revelation 2:7, 11, 17, 26, 3:5, 12, 21) To all seven churches Jesus proclaims, "He who has an ear, let him hear what the Spirit says to the churches." (Revelation 2:7, 11, 17, 29, 3:6, 13, 22) Are we listening to what the Spirit is saying to us? Can we hear, or have we become deaf? Nothing could be more serious!

To the church of Sardis he spoke,

"I know your deeds, that you have a reputation that you are alive, but in reality you are dead. Wake up then, and strengthen what remains that was about to die, because I have not found your deeds complete in the sight of my God. Therefore, remember what you received and heard, and obey it, and repent. If you do not wake up, I will come like a thief, and you will never know at what hour I will come against you. Revelation 3:1-3 (NET)

Nothing is hidden from our Lord. He knows the true state of our hearts and he knows our deeds and the motivations behind them. We may be fooled about ourselves, but God knows the truth. He knows those who truly love him and those who have been deceived. Like the church of Sardis, Jesus knew the deeds of the church of Laodicea, and their hearts were lukewarm toward God, without love for him.

'**I know your deeds,** that you are neither cold nor hot. I wish you were either cold or hot! So **because you are lukewarm, and neither hot nor cold, I am going to vomit you out of my mouth!** Because you say, "I am rich and have acquired great wealth, and need nothing," but do not realize that you are wretched, pitiful, poor, blind, and naked, take my advice and buy gold from me refined by fire so you can become rich! Buy from me white clothing so you can be clothed and your shameful nakedness will not be exposed, and buy eye salve to put on your eyes so you can see! All those I love, I rebuke and discipline. So be earnest and repent! Revelation 3:15-19 (NET)

And to the church of Ephesus he directly accuses them of forsaking their first love for him.

Yet I hold this against you: **You have forsaken your first love.** Remember the height from which you have fallen! **Repent and do the things you did at first.** If you do not repent, I will come to you and remove your lampstand from its place. Revelation 2:4-5 (NIV)

This is the church where Paul wrote, "Praise be to the God and Father of our Lord Jesus Christ, who has blessed us in the heavenly realms with every spiritual blessing in Christ." Ephesians 1:3 (NIV) They had everything. And apparently, at first, they did love God above all else. But their love waned and they eventually forsook their first love and replaced it with a love for other things.

197

Love is a choice. Love is always a choice. We may have a compelling desire to love someone, such as our newfound mate or our newborn child. But our love for them will be tested. For example, what happens when they are not so loving in return? What happens to our love when we realize that we cannot do all of the things we used to do before marriage or before having children? Our love will be tested when we find that to love requires of us to give up our own desires for the desires and needs of others. Love gets difficult when we have to forgo our own comforts or even suffer for the sake of another. In like manner, we choose to love God. It is great if we have warm heartfelt feelings. Realize that the choice may be mainly motivated by the pursuit of pleasurable feelings. But the true test of our love for God comes when we love sacrificially for the one we love. Jesus suffered the rejection of those he loved, even to the point of death. And he did this all out of his decisive, obedient love for his heavenly Father. Our love for God is no different. Genuine love for God is borne out in our sacrificial living for God, not in the pleasantries of life, but in the difficulties.

Therefore, since we are surrounded by such a great cloud of witnesses, let us throw off everything that hinders and the sin that so easily entangles, and let us run with perseverance the race marked out for us. Let us fix our eyes on Jesus, the author and perfecter of our faith, who for the joy set before him endured the cross, scorning its shame, and sat down at the right hand of the throne of God. **Consider him who endured such opposition from sinful men, so that you will not grow weary and lose heart.**

In your struggle against sin, you have not yet resisted to the point of shedding your blood. Hebrews 12:1-4 (NIV)

In our pursuit to love God, let us "not grow weary and lose heart".

Reflection Questions

How did you first come to the Lord? What motivated you to seek him and follow him? What were your heartfelt motivations?

How did you first follow him? Describe your disciplines and actions.

How has your walk with God changed over the years? Has the change been good or bad? Have you become more thankful and humble, or more self-centered and prideful?

How have you had to persevere in your faith in order to love God as a first priority? What have you had to give up in order to obediently follow him and love him?

Made in the USA
Middletown, DE
20 May 2022

66013776R00116